AFRICA: PROGRESS & PROBLEMS

POVERTY AND ECONOMIC ISSUES

AFRICA: PROGRESS & PROBLEMS

POVERTY AND ECONOMIC ISSUES

Tunde Obadina

Mason Crest Publishers
Philadelphia

Frontispiece: After a severe drought in 2000, this Ethiopian woman and her emaciated son traveled four days to a feeding center in Danan. According to the UN World Food Programme, approximately 25,000 people in Africa die from starvation each day.

Produced by OTTN Publishing, Stockton, New Jersey

Mason Crest Publishers
370 Reed Road
Broomall, PA 19008
www.masoncrest.com

3 5 7 9 8 6 4 2

Library of Congress Cataloging-in-Publication Data

Obadina, Tunde.
  Poverty and economic issues in Africa / Tunde Obadina.
      p. cm. — (Africa, progress and problems)
  Includes bibliographical references and index.
  ISBN-13: 978-1-59084-953-8
  ISBN-10: 1-59084-953-1
  1. Poverty—Africa. 2. Africa—Economic conditions. I. Title. II. Series.
  HC800.Z9P6263 2006
  339.4'6'096—dc22
                    2005023344

TABLE OF CONTENTS

Introduction	7
Poverty in Africa: An Overview	13
Africa's Fragile Environment	23
The Burden of History	26
Africa's Human Capital Deficit	51
Structural Impediments to Wealth Creation	65
Globalization: A Level Playing Field?	106
The Search for Solutions	114
Conclusion	119
Glossary	123
Further Reading	126
Internet Resources	127
Index	129

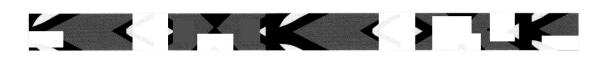

≋ AFRICA: PROGRESS & PROBLEMS ≋

AIDS AND HEALTH ISSUES

CIVIL WARS IN AFRICA

ECOLOGICAL ISSUES

EDUCATION IN AFRICA

ETHNIC GROUPS IN AFRICA

GOVERNANCE AND LEADERSHIP
IN AFRICA

HELPING AFRICA HELP ITSELF:
A GLOBAL EFFORT

HUMAN RIGHTS IN AFRICA

ISLAM IN AFRICA

THE MAKING OF MODERN AFRICA

POPULATION AND OVERCROWDING

POVERTY AND ECONOMIC ISSUES

RELIGIONS OF AFRICA

THE PROMISE OF TODAY'S AFRICA

by Robert I. Rotberg

Today's Africa is a mosaic of effective democracy and desperate despotism, immense wealth and abysmal poverty, conscious modernity and mired traditionalism, bitter conflict and vast arenas of peace, and enormous promise and abiding failure. Generalizations are more difficult to apply to Africa or Africans than elsewhere. The continent, especially the sub-Saharan two-thirds of its immense landmass, presents enormous physical, political, and human variety. From snow-capped peaks to intricate patches of remaining jungle, from desolate deserts to the greatest rivers, and from the highest coastal sand dunes anywhere to teeming urban conglomerations, Africa must be appreciated from myriad perspectives. Likewise, its peoples come in every shape and size, govern themselves in several complicated manners, worship a host of indigenous and imported gods, and speak thousands of original and five or six derivative common languages. To know Africa is to know nuance and complexity.

There are 53 nation-states that belong to the African Union, 48 of which are situated within the sub-Saharan mainland or on its offshore islands. No other continent has so many countries, political divisions, or members of the General Assembly of the United Nations. No other continent encompasses so many

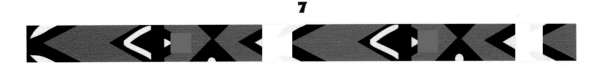

distinctively different peoples or spans such geographical disparity. On no other continent have so many innocent civilians lost their lives in intractable civil wars—12 million since 1991 in such places as Algeria, Angola, the Congo, Côte d'Ivoire, Liberia, Sierra Leone, and the Sudan. No other continent has so many disparate natural resources (from cadmium, cobalt, and copper to petroleum and zinc) and so little to show for their frenzied exploitation. No other continent has proportionally so many people subsisting (or trying to) on less than $1 a day. But then no other continent has been so beset by HIV/AIDS (30 percent of all adults in southern Africa), by tuberculosis, by malaria (prevalent almost everywhere), and by less well-known scourges such as schistosomiasis (liver fluke), several kinds of filariasis, river blindness, trachoma, and trypanosomiasis (sleeping sickness).

Africa is the most Christian continent. It has more Muslims than the Middle East. Apostolic and Pentecostal churches are immensely powerful. So are Sufi brotherhoods. Yet traditional African religions are still influential. So is a belief in spirits and witches (even among Christians and Muslims), in faith healing and in alternative medicine. Polygamy remains popular. So does the practice of female circumcision and other long-standing cultural preferences. Africa cannot be well understood without appreciating how village life still permeates the great cities and how urban pursuits engulf villages. Half if not more of its peoples live in towns and cities; no longer can Africa be considered predominantly rural, agricultural, or wild.

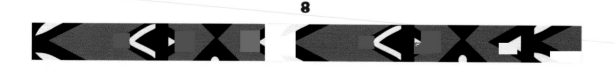

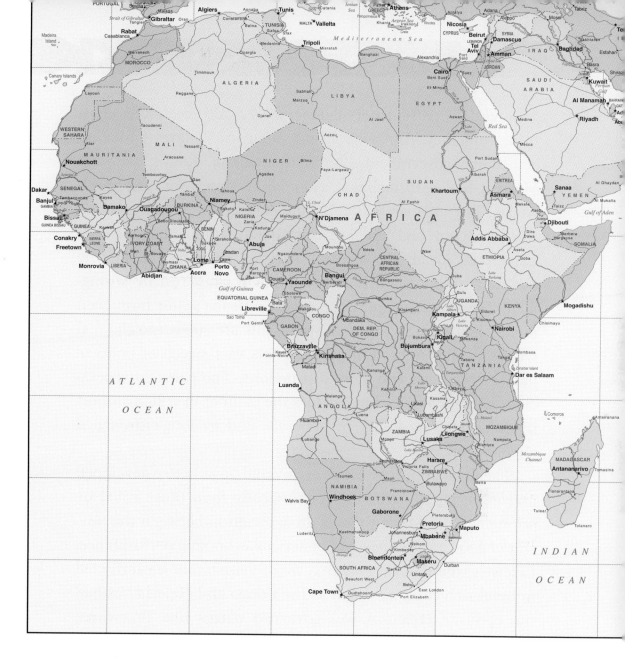

Political leaders must cater to both worlds, old and new. They and their followers must join the globalized, Internet-penetrated world even as they remain rooted appropriately in past modes of behavior, obedient to dictates of family, lineage, tribe, and ethnicity. This duality often results in democracy or at

least partially participatory democracy. Equally often it develops into autocracy. Botswana and Mauritius have enduring democratic governments. In Benin, Ghana, Kenya, Lesotho, Malawi, Mali, Mozambique, Namibia, Nigeria, Senegal, South Africa, Tanzania, and Zambia fully democratic pursuits are relatively recent and not yet sustainably implanted. Algeria, Cameroon, Chad, the Central African Republic, Egypt, the Sudan, and Tunisia are authoritarian entities run by strongmen. Zimbabweans and Equatorial Guineans suffer from even more venal rule. Swazis and Moroccans are subject to the real whims of monarchs. Within even this vast sweep of political practice there are still more distinctions. The partial democracies represent a spectrum. So does the manner in which authority is wielded by kings, by generals, and by long-entrenched civilian autocrats.

The democratic countries are by and large better developed and more rapidly growing economically than those ruled by strongmen. In Africa there is an association between the pursuit of good governance and beneficial economic performance. Likewise, the natural resource wealth curse that has afflicted mineral-rich countries such as the Congo and Nigeria has had the opposite effect in well-governed places like Botswana. Nation-states open to global trade have done better than those with closed economies. So have those countries with prudent managements, sensible fiscal arrangements, and modest deficits. Overall, however, the bulk of African countries have suffered in terms of reduced economic growth from the sheer fact of being tropical, beset by disease in an enervating climate

where there is an average of one trained physician to every 13,000 persons. Many lose growth prospects, too, because of the absence of navigable rivers, the paucity of ocean and river ports, barely maintained roads, and few and narrow railroads. Moreover, 15 of Africa's countries are landlocked, without comfortable access to relatively inexpensive waterborne transport. Hence, imports and exports for much of Africa are more expensive than elsewhere as they move over formidable distances. Africa is the most underdeveloped continent because of geographical and health constraints that have not yet been overcome, because of ill-considered policies, because of the sheer number of separate nation-states (a colonial legacy), and because of poor governance.

Africa's promise is immense, and far more exciting than its achievements have been since a wave of nationalism and independence in the 1960s liberated nearly every section of the continent. Thus, the next several decades of the 21st century are ones of promise for Africa. The challenges are clear: to alleviate grinding poverty and deliver greater real economic goods to larger proportions of people in each country, and across all 53 countries; to deliver more of the benefits of good governance to more of Africa's peoples; to end the destructive killing fields that run rampant across so much of Africa; to improve educational training and health services; and to roll back the scourges of HIV/AIDS, tuberculosis, and malaria. Every challenge represents an opportunity with concerted and bountiful Western assistance to transform the lives of Africa's vulnerable and resourceful future generations.

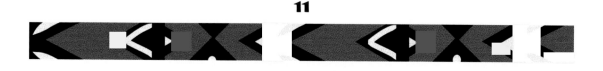

POVERTY IN AFRICA: AN OVERVIEW

ndependence came with high hopes in most African nations in the early 1960s. Departing colonial rulers transferred power to confident local elites and citizens who looked forward to prosperity and the material benefits of freedom. Given Africa's richness in natural resources, these expectations did not seem unreasonable. At the time, it was the less endowed and highly populated Asian countries that seemed to be at risk of spiraling turmoil. But things turned out differently. Over the past 50 years the images of Third World poverty shown in the West have changed from those of undernourished Indians and Chinese to those of hapless, starving Africans.

FALLING BEHIND

Africa has fallen behind the rest of the developing world. While many parts of Asia have seen rapid economic growth and a decline in mass deprivation, most people in Africa have languished in abject poverty. In 1960 the Republic

(Opposite) A baby in the Congo stands in the stony water hole where her mother washes laundry. The scope of poverty in sub-Saharan Africa is staggering: nearly half of the region's people live on less than a dollar a day.

of Korea was as poor as many African countries at the time. But in 2004 the country of 48 million people had a gross domestic product (GDP) that was 25 percent higher than the GDP of all of sub-Saharan Africa, with its 719 million people.

Africa started the 21st century as the poorest, most technologically backward, and most debt stressed region in the world. With 11 percent of the world's population, sub-Saharan Africa accounts for only 1 percent of the global GDP. It is the only continent to have become poorer since the mid-1980s. Poverty, as measured by the number of people living on less than $1 per day (all dollar amounts in this book refer to U.S. dollars), has risen steadily in sub-Saharan Africa during the past quarter century, although the proportion of the population living in abject want has remained largely unchanged. (Population growth accounts for the increase in absolute numbers of poor.) The number of people in the region who lived below the poverty line rose by almost 40 percent between 1990 and 2001, from 227 million to 313 million. Nearly 80 percent lived on less than $2 per day. Throughout the continent, countries are increasingly unable to provide the basic necessities of modern living, such as health care, clean water, and sanitation. Perhaps most disturbing, life expectancy has decreased in many African countries with the rise of the HIV/AIDS epidemic.

At a time of unprecedented prosperity in the world, Africa's economic stagnation and pervasive poverty have become matters of increasing international concern, drawing the attention of leaders within Africa as well as outside the continent. On current trends, it is unlikely that the United Nations Millennium Development Goals, which call for halving poverty by 2015, will be met in Africa. In contrast, East Asia has already achieved many of the goals, and South Asia is on track to meeting them.

Poverty is broadly defined as the lack of means to provide basic material needs or comforts, and it can be viewed in absolute and relative terms. Absolute poverty refers to a level of subsistence at which certain minimum standards of living measured by nutrition, health, and shelter cannot be met. Relative poverty compares the living standard of the lowest segment of society with that of the rest of the population. Some argue that all poverty beyond want of life-sustaining food is relative since there is no "absolute" standard fixed in time and location. What we consider to be necessities of life in the 21st century, such as clean water, water-flush sanitation, schooling, and health services, were luxuries two centuries ago—if they were available at all. Our perception of poverty is continuously being adapted and augmented as technological changes take place. So, abject poverty is relative to a minimum standard of living that we believe all human beings should be entitled to in today's advanced global community.

As poverty relates to access to the basic benefits of technological advancement, its persistence in Africa reflects the failure of technological development in the continent. This book explores the main reasons why sub-Saharan African nations have made so little progress in creating the wealth needed for the material well-being of their inhabitants.

Despite its plentiful natural resources, Africa had a weak starting point in the race for development. After gaining independence, Africans struggled with the legacies of the slave trade and colonialism. They inherited weak political institutions run by elites that were more interested in looting national treasuries or pursuing other narrow interests than in mobilizing resources to transform their materially backward societies. The ensuing post-colonial political turbulence, including numerous civil wars and military coups, created environments that stifled economic growth. Many African countries now find themselves caught in a poverty trap. Poor governance and instability impede economic growth and poverty reduction, and the resulting lack of prosperity pushes people to seek illegal ways to become rich.

DIFFERENT PERSPECTIVES ON POVERTY IN AFRICA

This appalling situation has led some people to believe that poverty is self-perpetuating. African states are seen as being simply too poor and corrupt to free themselves from underdevelopment, and therefore as needing to be rescued by the Western world. This view of poverty as a vicious circle is integral to development economics, which identifies the major predicament of poor nations as lack of capital due to inadequate savings and corruption.

According to this perspective, the solution to poverty lies mainly in the provision of foreign aid and debt relief, as well as in persuading African rulers to be more honest. However, over the past 50 years some very poor nations have managed to achieve significant levels of economic growth and poverty reduction with little foreign aid under governments that were as corrupt as those in the African countries that have failed to prosper.

Some commentators have seen the lack of progress in sub-Saharan Africa in this fast-changing world as evidence that its people inherently lack the abilities or inclinations for material advancement. Others believe that Third World poverty is something that the rich "superior" world—the West—is inflicting on poor weaker nations. This latter view, popular among African nationalists and anti-capitalists of all varieties, is as mistaken as the racist one.

History teaches us that poverty is not inescapable. If it were, there would be no rich countries, as every society that is now wealthy was once, not so long ago, as impoverished as Africa. The differences between poor and rich nations are not in the inherent abilities of their people, but in the opportunities that each has had and their ability to exploit those opportunities. What separates a poor illiterate farmer in Africa and a university professor in the United States is not necessarily that one has a superior intellect, but that their lives offered them different opportunities and choices. Of course, people with similar backgrounds faced with equal opportunities can have unequal outcomes because of differences in their individual abilities and inclinations.

In the case of illiterate African farmers struggling to make a living from infertile land, the main reason they remain poor is lack of opportunities that could enable them to improve their circumstances. They have few choices. This situation is tragic because global advancements in human knowledge, especially in science and technology, have greatly expanded the opportunities available to people in different parts of the world to improve the quality of their lives.

The increasing integration of economies around the world, largely resulting from human innovation and technological progress, has offered extensive opportunities for individuals and nations to tap into more and larger markets around the world. This process, known as globalization, has meant that people of all races and regions have access to more capital, technology, and cheaper imports, as well as larger markets to sell their goods and services. The Asian countries that have moved from poverty to newly industrialized economies achieved the transformation largely by tapping the opportunities offered by globalization. Arguably the most important opportunity has been the transfer of technology. Technology, in this sense, is the information and methodology necessary for efficient production of goods. The movement of technology from one country to another occurs in different ways, such as education, training, foreign investment, and extraction from imports. It is through advances in technology that poor nations have been able to create new industries,

South African entrepreneur Mthembeni Mkhize founded a company in Pretoria that manufactures vinyl products for the automobile industry. Mkize's company has gained major customers such as Ford, Toyota, and Daimler Chrysler. But its success is unusual for African firms, relatively few of which have managed to compete effectively in the global market.

generate new jobs, and generally achieve the economic growth necessary to reduce poverty.

We should bear in mind that people are not born with technological capabilities. The know-how is learned and transmitted from generation to generation. If America were somehow emptied of all its educational institutions and parents stopped teaching their children, the country would soon return to the Stone Age in its technological capabilities.

UNEVEN BENEFITS OF GLOBALIZATION

Africa has not benefited from globalization as much as other regions. In particular, it has not made much progress in adopting modern technology. Few firms in Africa outside of multinationals have the technological capacity to compete effectively in the global market. Some African leaders blame this situation on the rich nations, which they feel are seeking to keep the region underdeveloped in order to exploit its resources. This is a simplistic view of how the global economy works. Globalization is essentially based on market forces. This means that the flow of resources, including technological knowledge, is largely determined by the interaction of supply and demand and the relative prices of goods and services. Basically, resources flow to where their owners expect to get the biggest return. The market thereby promotes competition between individuals or firms as both buyers and sellers.

The developing nations that have achieved rapid economic growth during the past 50 years have been those that have been able to make the global market work for them. Asian producers used opportunities offered by the global economy, including trade, foreign investment, and technology, to accumulate assets (factories and equipment) and build up human capital (human skills and abilities) to produce goods and services that people want at prices that are competitive. By using their low-cost skilled labor to outperform high-cost producers, these countries have debunked the notion that underdeveloped nations are intrinsically at a disadvantage in economic competition with developed countries.

Africans have fared poorly in the global market largely because their governments have prevented them from exploiting many of the opportunities of globalization. Their rulers have failed to provide the enabling framework for citizens to increase their productive capacities. Most economists agree that Africa has been held back by bad governance. People in Africa have been unfortunate to live under governments that exercise power in ways that handicap broad sections of the population, often to enable privileged elites to enjoy the fruits of globalization without personal effort. Incompetent governments have severely restricted the freedom of individuals and firms to make decisions on the use of their properties and other resources in ways that serve their own interests.

Bad governance is manifest in many ways, including the following:

* ❋ Rulers failing in their primary responsibility to protect life and private property from crooked officials and criminals so that individuals and firms may safely and confidently create wealth.

* ❋ Governments mounting regulations—from absurdly lengthy procedures for starting new businesses to burdensome tax requirements and costly import clearance processes—that impede the ability of entrepreneurs to operate efficiently.

* ❋ Public resources that could have been invested in social services and infrastructure being stolen by corrupt officials or wasted in propping up indebted state enterprises.

* ❋ Governments erecting barriers against foreign trade and investment.

It is instructive that many of the impoverished African nations most in need of new investments, new enterprises, and new jobs also rank among the most difficult places in the world to do business. In trying to understand the failure of development in most parts of Africa, we need to look at how poor governance and technological backwardness have weighed down the region. This is not to suggest that there are not other factors, natural and external, that have hindered material progress in Africa.

Much of the continent suffers from environmental degradation, such as desertification, erosion, and declining soil fertility. Rainfall is erratic, while harsh climatic and ecological conditions make many areas susceptible to pests and diseases. African countries have also been held back by some inequities in the global trading system. For instance, farming subsidies paid to agricultural producers in industrialized nations give them unfair advantages in the international commodity markets and harm farmers in the developing world.

Nevertheless, technological backwardness, poor governance, and lack of economic freedom remain the major root causes of underdevelopment in Africa. Modern technology could go some way to ease many of Africa's environmental challenges. Countries with expanding production capacities benefit most from new opportunities.

However, when considering African poverty and stagnation, it is important that we bear in mind that Africa is not a homogeneous entity, but a vast continent comprising more than 50 states with varying challenges. The broad trends of underachievement in Africa often mask significant differences across the continent. For instance, while most African countries have recorded poor economic growth in recent years, since the mid-1990s 15 African countries have consistently averaged GDP growth of more than 6 percent per year. While the per capita income of Africa's least developed nations falls well below the average for developing nations, some countries, like Mauritius, South Africa, and Botswana, have income levels well above the average and surpass those of even China and India. There are major differences between relatively more developed African countries, like South Africa,

Technology in African countries is concentrated in urban centers, which have access to infrastructure. Telecenters, like this one in Senegal, provide phones for the public.

and the least developed ones, such as Sierra Leone, in terms of levels of technology and quality of governance.

Similarly, the view that Africa has made little or no progress during the past 30 years can be misleading. While the living conditions for the vast majority of Africans remain harsh and substandard, there have nevertheless been some significant improvements in the continent. Since 1990, for example, 40 of the 48 countries in sub-Saharan Africa have held multi-party elections, in contrast to the earlier decades when the continent was dominated by dictators. There have also been significant improvements in some important social indicators, such as levels of immunization, infant mortality, literacy, and secondary school enrollment. Throughout Africa there is visibly greater access to services, such as motorized transportation, television and radio broadcasts, and telephone services. And many more modern goods, from clothing and soap to plastics and kitchen utensils, have become affordable.

Africa's problem is not that it has stood still, but that it has not been able to keep pace with world progress. The rest of this book will explore in some detail how and why this has happened and what is being done to remedy the situation.

AFRICA'S FRAGILE ENVIRONMENT

Most of the poorest places in the world are located close to the equator. They lie in the tropical and semi-tropical zones, between the tropic of Cancer and the tropic of Capricorn. These are very hot regions that experience torrential rains and widespread dangerous diseases. Many of Africa's impoverished nations fall within this location. For those who believe that geography is a fundamental cause of differences in the prosperity between countries, Africa's difficult physical environment, climate, and ecology point to an obvious explanation of its failure to develop.

THE IMPACT OF HARSH CLIMATES AND DELICATE ECOLOGY

Some writers believe that constant favorable temperatures make people in tropical countries more prone to complacency. They are more inclined to stay outdoors, and compared with those living in temperate zones, they lack the impetus to innovate building materials and methods for creating shelter to maintain comfort from cold, harsh weather. Nature, it seems, dealt Europe more favorable conditions—cold that keeps down pathogens and pests, while encouraging innovative use of natural forces to generate energy to heat and power homes.

The geographic explanation of the wealth of nations is questionable, but there is no doubt that Africa has, over recent decades, experienced growing environmental degradation, such as deforestation, desertification, soil erosion, declining soil fertility, loss of biodiversity, and depletion of fresh water, which limits the potential for economic growth. Although Africa is often portrayed as a land with natural advantage for agricultural production, nature has, in fact, placed considerable limitations on farming there. Only about one-fifth of Africa's surface area is potential farmland, and about half of this is made up of soil high in iron and aluminum, which hinder cultivated plants.

An African farmer surveys the damage to his crops from soil erosion. Much of Africa's farmland is already of marginal quality, and environmental degradation presents an increasing threat.

Climate experts expect climatic and ecological conditions in Africa to deteriorate in coming years, placing increasing pressure on the region's growing population. A 2005 report by the United Nations Food and Agriculture Organization said that the severest impact of climate change was likely to be in sub-Saharan African countries, which are the least able to handle the impact of worsening conditions. The report explained that there are 2.7 billion acres (1.1 billion hectares) of land in Africa with a growing period of less than 120 days. Climate change could, by 2080, result in an expansion of this area by 5 to 8 percent.

Africa's fragile environment has been further threatened in places by poor land management and inadequate investment in technology to achieve more efficient production systems. Overly intensive farming and overgrazing have led to depletion of soil, forest, and water resources and resulted in declining yields. With increased population pressure, many farmers have abandoned the traditional practice of shifting cultivation to maintain soil fertility. African farmers also use much less fertilizer per acre than growers in other developing regions. Similarly, the use of pesticides and herbicides to control pests, diseases, and weeds is minimal, and levels of irrigation in the region are very low, given the arid conditions.

THE BURDEN OF HISTORY

The momentum for the modern economic development of the world can be traced back to the Industrial Revolution that began in England during the middle of the 18th century and then spread over the next half century to Europe and America. This revolution entailed a complex of radical social and economic changes, including the extensive mechanization of production, which brought about rapid industrial growth and transformed the lives of the people.

At the time when people in England began to undergo these changes, the differences between their living standards and those of the inhabitants of Africa were not huge. In 1700 the gross domestic product of the United Kingdom was $10.7 billion, amounting to some $1,250 per person, while the GDP of Africa was $24.4 billion, equivalent to $293 per person. By 1820 Britain's GDP had more than tripled, to $36.2 billion; Africa's GDP, by contrast, showed only a marginal increase to $31 billion. Over time, the gap between per capita income in Britain and Africa has widened: today the ratio stands at more than 14 to 1, whereas in 1700 it was only 4 to 1.

There is little agreement among historians on why the industrial revolution occurred in Europe and not in other parts of the world. Various factors have been suggested, including a temperate physical environment, good governance, high population density, and an entrepreneurial, individualistic culture. The absence of many of these factors in Africa may also explain why an industrial revolution did not occur there. Although the gap in levels of economic production in Europe and Africa in the 18th century was not as huge as it is today, there were nevertheless fundamental differences between societies in the two regions.

THE SLAVE TRADE

While technological innovations such as steam power were propelling rapid changes in the way that people in Europe lived and worked, the socio-political environment in Africa was quite hostile to any kind of human material progress. One of the main features of many African communities was the prevalence of slave trading. The domestic use and sale of slaves in Africa goes back many centuries, but it was the transatlantic slave trade between the 15th and 19th centuries that marked the height of the trade in African chattel. Between 1450 and 1870 an estimated 12 million Africans were shipped from Africa to the Americas and the Caribbean, with the largest number traded between the late 18th and early 19th centuries—the period of economic blossoming in Europe and the United States.

The slave trade had profound economic, social, cultural, and psychological impacts on African people and societies, which undermined their prospects for development. Through the trade Africa lost a significant portion of its young and able-bodied population. Besides the people carried abroad, countless numbers of

This woodcut depicts the crowded deck of a slave ship called the *Wildfire*, which brought slaves to Florida in 1800. The transatlantic slave trade depleted Africa of valuable labor, hampering economic development on the continent. At the same time, it helped spur production and the accumulation of capital in Britain and the Americas.

Africans were killed or maimed in the numerous raids and inter-communal wars waged to procure slaves. The fighting and rampant kidnappings fueled hostility and suspicion between communities; distrust was a basic requirement for survival. The slave trade arrested and distorted the cultural development of African societies. It affected the meaning that people gave to the world and their place within it. The increased uncertainty of life gave added force to superstition as people sought salvation and protection from the spiritual world. The psychological impact of the dehumanizing trade was crippling, and the constant anxiety caused by perpetual fear of capture was debilitating. All in all, the slave trade fostered an environment that was opposite to that of Europe. Freedom and social trust are essential for economic investment and scientific development.

Profits from the transatlantic slave trade helped fuel industrial investment in Britain. Slavery also gave value to the New World colonies, which were important sources of goods for Britain's emergent capitalists. Whereas Europeans invested their gains from the slave trade in laying the foundation of a powerful economic empire, the African kings and traders who supplied most of the men and women taken from Africa did not invest their fortunes. Items imported from Europe during those dark centuries were consumption goods or weapons for waging more slave-generating wars and raids. There was little to nothing imported in the way of capital that could have been used to enhance the productive capacity of Africa's communities.

Indeed, the slave trade seriously undermined African economies. The loss in human resources weakened labor-intensive agricultural production. The few existing manufacturing activities were either destroyed or greatly impaired. Importation of relatively cheap European textiles, for instance, crippled local cloth production. Samuel Johnson wrote in the late 19th century about Yorubaland in today's Nigeria: "Before the period of intercourse with Europeans, all articles made of iron and steel, from weapons of war to pins and needles, were of home manufacture; but the cheaper and more finished articles of European make, especially cutlery, though less durable are fast displacing home-made wares."

IMPACT OF COLONIAL RULE

With the decline and eventual abolition of the transatlantic slave trade and slavery in the New World, European interest in Africa focused more on the cultivation of primary products in the continent, to be used as raw materials for industries in Europe as well as items for exotic consumption. From around the 1880s to the start of the First World War in 1914, rival European powers grabbed different portions of Africa to colonize in what became known as the "Scramble for Africa."

There is much disagreement among historians regarding the impact of colonialism on Africa's economies. Some writers view it as an intrinsically negative experience for Africans, whose labor and resources were exploited by European supremacists in ways that hindered Africa's capacity for growth. They see a link between colonial rule and the structural underdevelopment of the colonial and post-colonial economies—a condition supposedly engineered by the imperial powers in the interest of their own Western economies. For these writers, colonialism was a totally cynical endeavor by which underdeveloped regions of the world were incorporated into the international capitalist economy as suppliers of raw materials and markets for manufactured goods. The Guyanese historian Walter Rodney, in his influential book *How Europe Underdeveloped Africa*, argued that under colonialism the only things that evolved were dependency and underdevelopment. As far as Rodney and other critics of European imperial rule are concerned, the only positive development in colonialism was its ending.

Quite a different perspective on colonial rule is provided by many other historians who view colonialism as a blessing for Africa, helping to liberate its people from endemic backwardness and introduce them to a modern world. Western historians like the Cambridge academic D. K. Fieldhouse have argued that the societies that were colonized in the late 19th century lacked the social and economic organization to transform themselves into modern states able to develop advanced economies. Had they not become European possessions, they would probably have remained unchanged—or, at the very least, much more time would have passed before they began to see technological innovation and economic advancement. Economist Peter Bauer boldly asserted that "far from the West having caused the poverty in the Third World, contact with the West has been the principal agent of material progress there."

Leaving aside the moral issues raised by the imperial powers' use of conquest and coercion, the effects of European colonial domination of communities in Africa and elsewhere in the

In this early 20th century photo, British administrators in Nigeria meet with tribal messengers. British colonizers used indirect rule in Nigeria, relying largely on existing local rulers and systems to maintain order.

world were not as simple as both the critics and apologists would have us believe. Clearly, empire building was driven by the political and economic self-interest of the European nations. It facilitated the production and extraction of surpluses for external markets, while paying little attention to the development of the domestic market.

There were differences in the colonization strategies of the imperial powers, with different impacts on the subject peoples. At one extreme, there were those whose sole interest was plundering the resources of colonized lands, exemplified by the Belgian colonization of the Congo. In contrast, elsewhere in Africa imperial powers introduced institutions that served to incorporate their colonies into the global economic system. They established a legal framework in which capitalist relations could operate and domestic markets could be built. To meet their economic and administrative needs, colonial powers built some infrastructure, such as railways and roads, to ferry export commodities and introduced modern financial systems to facilitate commerce. They also established the rule of law and educated some of the local people to help them administer the colonies.

Many of these positive developments took place mainly toward the end of the colonial period and were concentrated in a few areas in each country. The degree of modernization varied between the different colonies. For instance, the Portuguese added very little to their African possessions. After gaining independence in 1975, Mozambique had only three dozen university graduates, whereas the French and British colonies were educationally much better equipped.

When African nations achieved independence in the early 1960s, the vast majority of the people were very poor. Only a small elite had access to modern amenities, such as electricity, potable water, sanitation, an adequate education, and health care. Nevertheless, the per capita national income of most newly free

African states was higher than it had been before colonization. African countries were almost totally dependent on agricultural production, and farmers in many countries struggled to cultivate enough food to meet the nutritional needs of their people. Yet as a result of colonialism, Africans were producing a wider range of commodities, including cocoa, yam, cassava, and rubber.

A few modern industries were established in colonial Africa, mainly during its closing years and mainly in the cities. A small number of large factories were set up and operated by foreigners, chiefly Europeans, while indigenous entrepreneurs established small- or medium-scale concerns. For instance, Nigeria in the 1950s had one of the world's biggest veneer and plywood mills. There were also groundnut, palm oil, and rubber mills and factories making cigarettes, soap, and margarine. Factories owned by

Construction of the Djibouti–Addis Ababa railway, which is still in use today, was begun in 1897 by the British and completed 18 years later by a joint English-French company. While European colonial powers were motivated by self-interest, they did build some infrastructure, and introduce institutions, that facilitated economic development in parts of Africa.

Nigerians included textile mills, singlet (undershirt) factories, and a ceramics factory. Smaller concerns produced an assortment of products, such as traditional crafts, furniture, garments, shoes, bread, bottled beverages, roasted coffee, and spices.

During the colonial era, foreign investment in Africa remained low, as European capitalists were not motivated to invest in the colonies. With large pools of cheap labor in the metropolitan centers allowing plenty of room for industrial expansion at home, there was no need to look elsewhere. Despite this, the colonial period in Africa saw significant growth in modern production. Even when hampered by a shortage of financial capital, management skills, and technological know-how, the era of colonial manufacturing nevertheless marked the early stages of the application of modern technology and the factory system to the production of goods.

A South African entrepreneur constructs a chair by hand in his factory. Where the size of markets is small—as is the case throughout much of Africa—it makes little sense to invest in expensive machinery that could increase production efficiency or capacity because prospects for recouping the investment are slim.

Arguably the most profound impact of European expansion in Africa was the introduction of capitalism. By capitalism we mean an economic system in which the means of production, distribution, and exchange are privately owned and operated for profit. Colonial rule quashed political freedom, but by incorporating the colonies in the global capitalist system it expanded economic freedom among sections of the colonized. Under capitalism individuals are free to employ the three factors of production—land, labor, and capital—to produce goods and services, which are traded in a market to gain profit. The system is based on self-interest and private property, especially the idea that the owners of capital have legal rights that entitle them to earn profit as a reward for putting their capital at risk in some form of economic activity. This was in sharp contrast to the pre-colonial system in Africa, in which the individual's interests were subsumed to those of the community, keeping the means of production under traditional influences.

In opening up Africa to international trade, European powers not only designated the continent as a supplier of primary commodities for Western factories, but also gave Africans access to enlarged markets, which enabled greater economic specialization and division of labor. The introduction of capitalism in Africa also created the conditions for the development of African entrepreneurial classes. Entrepreneurs are vital to capitalist economic development, as they are the people who assume the organization, management, and risks of business enterprises. They are the individuals, operating on their own or in firms, who coordinate the factors of production to produce goods and services for sale in markets.

The Austrian economist Joseph Schumpeter explained that entrepreneurship is the driving force of modern economic growth. Entrepreneurship has been defined as "the manifest ability and willingness of individuals, on their own, in teams within and outside existing organizations, to perceive and create new economic opportunities (new products, new production methods, new organizational schemes and new product-market combinations) and to introduce their ideas in the market in the face of uncertainty and other obstacles, by making decisions on location, form and the use of resources and institutions." Entrepreneurship is, hence, a behavioral characteristic of a person. Capitalist economic development essentially involves people creating new products or finding new combinations of the factors of production to achieve better ways to meet existing demand. A farmer who introduces a new hybrid seed or employs a new appliance to boost his output in a manner that increases his profit is being entrepreneurial.

Entrepreneurs set up firms, which are the basic agents in a market economy. It is firms that bring the factors of production together to produce goods and services. Firms supervise the process of wealth creation—from buying raw materials to organizing the marketing and distribution of the final product. It is the firm that puts new techniques and ideas to practical use, and it is the firm that harnesses human capital to the best advantage.

The emergence of the firm is one of the most important developments of capitalism and arguably the most crucial introduction into the African colonies. Unlike a subsistence farmer or survival entrepreneur, a firm attempts to make profit and expand as an entity. Whereas producers in traditional society engaged in production to meet their immediate needs and passed on any surpluses to higher authorities, such as the monarch, the firm engages in economic activities to make profit. And in order to maintain or increase its profit level in the face of competition, the firm must invest to increase its productivity. In traditional society, producers had little incentive to invest in expansion, since most or all surplus production was appropriated by others.

It is difficult, even impossible, to know how Africa would

have developed economically if it had not been colonized. Looking at those territories that were not subject to European rule does not provide any cohesive picture. Ethiopia, Africa's oldest independent nation—which with the exception of a five-year occupation by Mussolini's Italy has never been colonized—was one of the poorest and least developed countries in Africa at the end of the colonial era. In 1950 its GDP per capita was less than a third of the average for Africa as a whole. Another African country that escaped colonization was Liberia, Africa's oldest republic. This nation, founded by freed American slaves, achieved higher economic output than many colonized African countries. In 1950 its GDP was roughly 25 percent higher than the average for Africa, though still less than levels reached in Senegal, Mauritius, Gabon, and South Africa. Most of Liberia's wealth was, however, concentrated in the hands of the descendants of freed American slaves who applied Western technology.

INDEPENDENCE AND POLITICAL INSTABILITY

At the time of political independence, most African economies were more buoyant than they are now. Relative to conditions today, many African countries had less corrupt political leadership committed to development and a reasonably efficient, independent civil service. This was reflected in the fact that, during the first half of the 20th century, Africa experienced more rapid economic growth than did Asia. During the initial years of political independence, agricultural production rose steadily and industry expanded due to increased foreign investment and domestic participation in the industrial sector. Unfortunately, by the early 1970s many African economies had begun to run into trouble as the result of deteriorating political environments.

The institutions of governance established during colonial rule began to crumble under the weight of conflicts between rival ethnic-based groups competing for power and access to economic resources. Within a decade of independence about a third of the governments in Africa were toppled in military coups. Africa became the most conflict-ridden region in the world. According to the Organization of African Unity, 26 conflicts erupted in Africa between 1963 and 1994, affecting 61 percent of the continent's population.

Many explanations have been offered for the collapse of democracy in post-colonial Africa. The failure of the states to flourish has been blamed on the inappropriateness of the European models of government installed by the imperial powers. It is said that the institutions were not only alien, but also incompatible with traditional African culture. Further, it is claimed that the states created by the Europeans forced together many incompatible ethnic groups. The new states thereby inevitably fell apart once the colonial authorities departed.

Looters in Lesotho run across the main street in the capital, Maseru. In 1998, suspecting a military coup, South Africa sent soldiers to rescue the flagging Lesotho government. This force met with resistance from the local military, and fighting ensued. Political instability discourages investment in Africa.

Others have argued that Africa's governance crisis did not stem from the incompatibility of Western democracy with African culture or the ethnic mix of the continent's young nations. For instance, some World Bank researchers have argued that nations that are either ethnically homogeneous or highly diverse should be less prone to civil war than those with a dominant ethnic group and minority. Ibrahim Elbadawi and Nicolas Sambanis argue that Africa's ethnic diversity should help, not impede, the emergence of stable development, as it necessitates inter-group bargaining processes. However, in Africa all types of national compositions, from ethnically homogeneous Somalia to highly diverse Nigeria, have suffered civil wars and internal strife.

As Elbadawi and Sambanis conclude in their World Bank study of civil strife in Africa: "Deep political and economic development failures—not tribalism or ethnic hatred—are the root causes of Africa's problems." Africa's development and nation-building crises are largely the results of the scramble for wealth and power by its emergent elites, who have used ethnicity and other divisive means to marshal popular support for their own ends. Throughout the continent, the state became embroiled in the struggles between competing groups wrestling for control of limited national resources.

The political, social, and governmental instability generated by the conflicts has subverted Africa's investment climate (the specific factors shaping the opportunities and incentives for entrepreneurs and firms to invest productively, create jobs, and expand). This has had dire consequences on the ability of African economies to grow and reduce poverty. Entrepreneurs are much less likely to invest their time and resources when factors beyond their control make the risk of failure high.

Political instability and civil strife have also taken a huge toll on affected nations and their neighbors. Large amounts of resources that could have been used to develop infrastructure and public utilities were sunk into increasing military spending. For instance, it is estimated that resources diverted from development uses by conflict amounted to $1 billion per year in Central Africa and more than $800 million per year in West Africa. Conflict also led to the destruction of much of the already inadequate physical assets of affected countries, such as houses, schools, hospitals, and various infrastructures.

AFRICAN STATES ASSUME COMMAND OVER ECONOMIES

Most governments in Africa, as elsewhere in the Third World, maintained direct control of their national economies after attaining independence. This partly reflected an ideological inclination toward socialism prevalent not only in the developing world but also in Europe. It was assumed that the state had a central role to play in driving national economic growth. Given the weakness of indigenous private sectors, only the state appeared to have the ability to accumulate capital to invest in rapid development. Many Western economists at the time supported state-led development strategies based on centralized economic planning. This approach also appealed to local politicians and administrators, as it provided a rationale for their control of the distribution of wealth.

African governments invested substantial sums of money establishing state-owned and -run enterprises in various sectors of their economies. Initially, the emergence of state factories gave nations the impression of undergoing industrial take-off. Governments also embarked on policies of nationalization of existing industries, leaving the state with a monopoly in various economic activities. However, with very few exceptions, this policy of direct state economic domination proved disastrous for African economies. Africa's state enterprises were poorly

Black South African squatters in Kempton Park, northeast of Johannesburg, 2001. When white landowners in Kempton Park refused to sell their land, the squatters were forcibly removed — reflecting the difficulties South Africa has encountered in trying to effect land reform through a "willing buyer, willing seller" approach.

managed, often by bureaucrats with little business acumen. Where professional managers were engaged, they were typically hampered by government interference. State enterprises became conduits for politicians and administrators to bleed their nation's coffers through various forms of corrupt activities.

As in other parts of the underdeveloped world, governments in Africa maintained control over the flow and use of the factors of production by private enterprise. In most African countries, ownership of land was vested in the state or traditional authorities. As it was not an easily tradable commodity, land was difficult for entrepreneurs to obtain in order to pursue economic activities. Furthermore, governments maintained restrictive labor laws, which sought to protect indigenous workers against exploitation but which in practice imposed constraints on employers.

Probably the most economically damaging aspect of statism was the restriction on capital. In economics, capital comprises the elements of production from which an income is derived. It is money or physical assets used to produce more wealth, such as factories and machinery or working capital comprising raw materials, components, and money. Unlike land, capital is mobile; unlike labor, it can be legitimately subjected to property rights. Capital is in many ways the most important determinant of economic growth. Every economically underdeveloped community or nation has land, which is a fairly fixed factor, and a supply of able-bodied people willing to work. Capital is the major variant. A nation's economic development and prosperity depend on the skill with which capital is combined with its labor to produce goods and services. The efficiency by which capital is applied in economic activity is the main determinant of labor productivity. Many of the differences in living standards across nations reflect differences in labor productivity.

Capitalists use capital to make money, much of which they then plow back into the means of production in order to make more money and capture a bigger slice of the market. This process of capital accumulation—the growth in the country's stock of capital assets, such as new factories, manufacturing machinery, and communications systems—is commonly referred to as investment in real capital. Growth in real capital is essential for economic development and increasing the prosperity of a nation. Capitalism is a system in which the means of production and distribution are wholly or mainly privately owned and development is proportional to the accumulation and reinvestment of profit.

One of the major tragedies in post-colonial Africa, as elsewhere in the underdeveloped world, was that government interventions in the economy systematically undermined the growth of capital. For instance, African governments maintained and tightened the foreign exchange regimes they inherited. Strict controls were imposed on the purchase and sale of foreign currencies, usually requiring all transactions to go through government agencies. Exchange rates fixed by the state tended to overvalue the local currency, which made the country's exports more expensive to foreign buyers and its imports cheaper to local consumers. This had devastating effects on agricultural incentives. It fueled corruption and led to wasteful foreign exchange allocation. By making food imports cheap, overvalued exchange regimes discouraged domestic producers. Farmers were unable to get higher prices for their produce because exporters received less for their foreign currency receipts than they would have gotten in the free market. If, for instance, the Ghanaian cedi were 10 to the dollar instead of 2 to the dollar, each pound of cocoa that sold for $2 would yield 20 cedis instead of just 4, enabling the exporter to pay the farmer more.

Governments tended to rationalize the high value placed on national currencies in nationalistic terms, presenting the strength of currency as an indication of national virility, but the practice amounted to a tax on export commodity producers, especially farmers. This and other monetary policies denied farmers the full benefits of their enterprises. It meant that they made little profit from their endeavors and became discouraged from reinvesting whatever profits they made to boost their production capacity.

In addition to discouraging exports and encouraging imports, overvalued currencies have been corrosive in moral and administrative terms. As demand for imported goods rose due to their relatively low prices, governments resorted to foreign exchange rationing, mainly in the form of issuance of import licenses and limits on the amounts and use of hard currencies purchased by individuals and firms. Throughout Africa and other developing regions, parallel markets arose where hard currencies could be

(continued on p. 46)

FREE MARKET CURRENCY

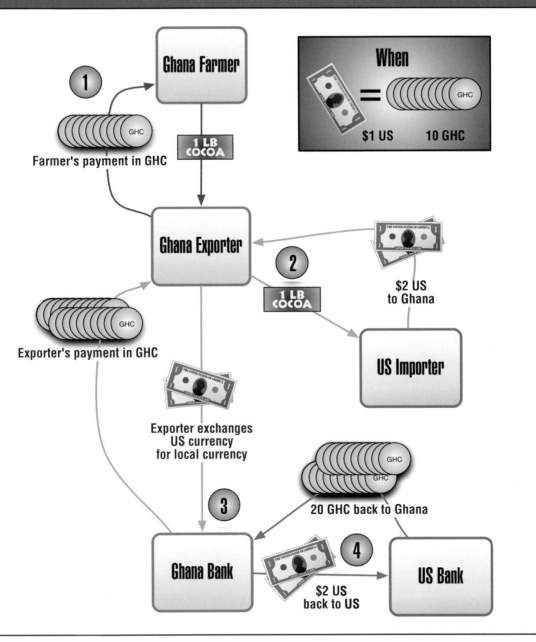

Ghana Farmer

①

Farmer's payment in GHC

When

$1 US = 10 GHC

1 LB COCOA

Ghana Exporter

②

$2 US to Ghana

1 LB COCOA

Exporter's payment in GHC

US Importer

Exporter exchanges US currency for local currency

20 GHC back to Ghana

③

Ghana Bank

④

$2 US back to US

US Bank

This highly simplified example illustrates one way in which local agricultural producers are hurt by an overvalued national currency. In each case the product—a pound of cocoa—is exported from Ghana to the United States for $2. But when the Ghanaian cedi (GHC) is artificially overvalued (opposite page), the transaction returns fewer cedis to the local economy than when the exchange rate is determined by market forces and more accurately reflects the cedi's real value (above). With the pound of cocoa yielding fewer cedis, the exporter must pay the farmer less.

OVERVALUED CURRENCY

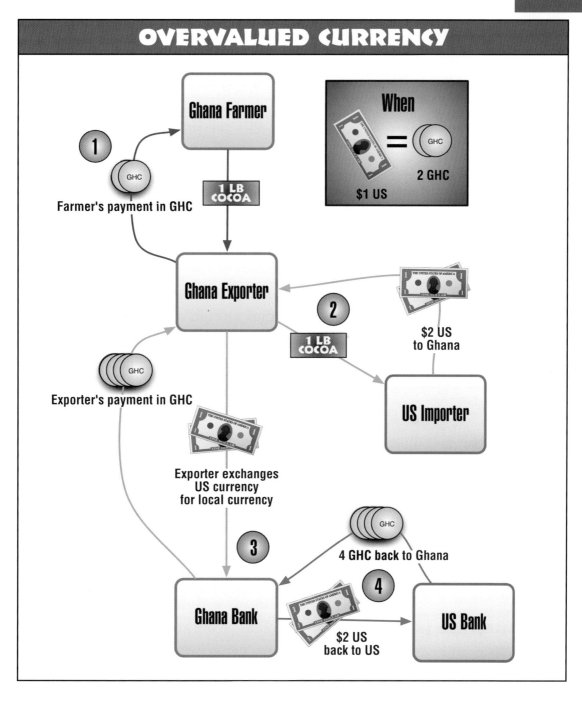

Ghana Farmer

When

$1 US = GHC

2 GHC

① Farmer's payment in GHC

GHC

1 LB COCOA

Ghana Exporter

② $2 US to Ghana

1 LB COCOA

Exporter's payment in GHC

GHC

US Importer

Exporter exchanges US currency for local currency

③

4 GHC back to Ghana

GHC

④

Ghana Bank

$2 US back to US

US Bank

CHART KEY

1.   Ghanaian farmer sells cocoa to exporter, is paid in cedis.
2.   Ghanaian exporter sells cocoa to U.S. importer, is paid in U.S. dollars.
3.   Exporter exchanges dollars for cedis at a bank in Ghana.
4.   Ghanaian bank, U.S. bank exchange Ghanaian-held dollars for U.S.-held cedis.

Gideon Gono, governor of the Reserve Bank of Zimbabwe, speaks at a press conference in 2005 concerning his country's decision to devalue its currency by 94 percent. Zimbabwe had been desperately short of foreign currency because of the disastrous rule of its longtime leader, Robert Mugabe, and because global donors pulled funding over disagreements with the policies of the Mugabe government.

bought and sold at market rates. The big differential between official and parallel exchange rates meant that people with access to import licenses and official foreign currencies were able to make huge and instant profits by trading their concessions in the parallel market. The system invariably gave rise to widespread abuse, as people became rich overnight simply because of their political or family connections to those controlling the official foreign exchange market.

By interfering in the free operation of the foreign exchange market, governments undermined the incentive system of productive capitalism. They discouraged export commodity producers while providing a strong incentive for unproductive elites to seek quick wealth by exploiting the artificial distortion in the currency market rather than assume the risks entailed in real wealth creation.

Besides ill-advised meddling in foreign exchange markets, other forms of economic intervention by African governments acted as disincentives for people and firms to enter into productive activities—and for those already so engaged to invest in the expansion of their businesses. For instance, the tendency of African governments to impose controls on the financial system, especially keeping interest rates low (supposedly to aid local producers), damaged the development of capital. Few people were prepared to lend money or deposit their assets in banks, making financial institutions unable to lend to businesses. Indeed, faced with high inflation, it was in the interest of wealthy individuals to transfer their assets abroad, where those assets could retain their value over time.

Interventionist governments also piled up regulations that made doing business in their countries extremely difficult. Even after years of economic liberalization, Africa remains arguably the most difficult place in the world to conduct business. Businesspeople face mountains of red tape to start a business, register property, and clear goods at ports.

POOR GOVERNANCE OBSTRUCTS DEVELOPMENT

If African governments have undermined economic development by what they have done, they have also undermined development by what they have failed to do. They have, for example, failed to adequately protect the lives and property of their citizens. In some countries state operatives have been among the biggest perpetrators of crime, especially the violation of property rights. African countries, with few exceptions, rank among the most corrupt in international probity indexes. In many countries, corruption permeates all levels of the state, from large-scale embezzlement by national leaders to petty bribe-taking by lower officials. A recent European Union report estimates that stolen African assets amounting to more than half of Africa's external debt are held in foreign bank accounts. In its Global Corruption Barometer 2004, a survey of 64 countries (including 5 in sub-Saharan Africa), Transparency International—a non-governmental organization devoted to fighting corruption—asked respondents whether officials had requested a bribe from them in the previous 12 months. Three African countries topped the list, with 52 percent of respondents from Cameroon, 36 percent from Kenya, and 32 percent from Nigeria saying they had been asked to pay a bribe. Other surveys have shown that official corruption is rife in most parts of Africa, with high proportions of citizens compelled to pay bribes to officials just to get by in life.

In recent years, Africans have suffered higher rates of violent crime than people from other regions. Southern, western, and central African countries rank among the countries with the highest rates of murder per capita. Surveys have shown that Africans report being burglarized more than people of other areas and that fraud is more common on the continent than in any place besides Eastern Europe. Criminal groups, often with the support of government officials, have been smuggling the continent's natural resources, such as oil, diamonds, and timber, to criminal syndicates in exchange for weapons. For example, in Nigeria's oil-rich Niger Delta region, criminal gangs and rebel militias have been stealing large quantities of crude oil from pipelines and using some of the proceeds to buy weapons. Much of the violence that has occurred in the region in recent years has been the result of turf wars between rival groups seeking to control oil theft. The situation is somewhat akin to the wars waged in previous centuries by African chiefs and merchants to secure slaves in exchange for weapons.

The combination of government meddling, political instability, and prolonged violence has created environments in Africa that are not conducive to private sector investment. Entrepreneurs and financial investors need to be confident about their prospects of success; they do not risk their assets unless they believe they have a reasonable chance of recovering their investment and making a profit. Freedom to make important economic decisions, along with assurance that their property rights will be protected against predatory individuals or groups, is a prerequisite. Investments in productive activities usually take several years to start yielding profits, so signs of

Exposed oil pipelines such as these have proved easy targets for Nigerian criminal gangs and rebel militia groups. Stolen oil helps fund these groups' weapons purchases, exacerbating violence in Nigeria's Niger Delta region.

future instability can deter investors. Entrepreneurs tend to have a long-term view of the development of their projects, often aspiring to build them into lasting establishments.

Lack of good governance in most African countries, especially the weak enforcement of property rights for a broad section of society, has negated incentives to invest or engage in productive activities. Individuals and firms have come to regard Africa as too risky a place to do business. Total capital inflows to sub-Saharan Africa as a percentage of GDP are lower than for other developing regions. This has not always been the case. In the early years of independence up until the early 1970s, Africa attracted a higher percentage of foreign direct investment (FDI) than did either Asia or Latin America. But by the year 2000, flows into Asia were 9 times higher and those into Latin America were 5.5 times higher than flows into Africa.

Unfortunately, it is not only foreigners who have been afraid to invest in African countries. Africa has the highest incidence of capital flight in the world, with an estimated 40 percent of private funds held outside the continent, compared with only 5 percent for South Asia, 6 percent for East Asia, and 10 percent for Latin America. The high rate of capital flight from Africa partly reflects looted funds stashed abroad by corrupt officials. But most importantly it indicates a serious lack of investor confidence among Africans. Large-scale corruption exists in other developing regions, but it appears that corrupt Asians and Latin Americans invest most of their loot at home, thereby contributing to the growth of domestic capital. Dishonest Africans bank most of their money abroad. Many honest Africans also choose to invest their hard-earned money overseas, where they believe it is safer. When Africans do invest at home, it tends to be in short-term commercial activities, such as trading.

AFRICA'S HUMAN CAPITAL DEFICIT

Africa has yet to produce a critical mass of skilled and highly trained workers capable of sustaining a technologically driven economy. Most economists agree that human capital—the collection of people's skills and abilities—is a major factor in differences in the wealth of nations. Generally, the more skilled and able a nation's workforce is, the greater its capacity to use modern technology to create wealth. Like physical capital, human capital is a stock of assets that yield income. Individuals and society build up human capital by investing in education, training, and medical care. Many studies have shown that education and training greatly raise a person's productivity and, thereby, his or her income. It is also clearly the case that a healthy person is likely to be more productive than one who is sick.

By every indicator of human capital, Africa is the least endowed of all regions of the world. Schooling levels are low. According to the United Nations Development Program's Human

Development Report 2004, the combined gross enrollment ratio for primary schools, secondary schools, and colleges and universities for sub-Saharan Africa in 2001–2002 was only 44 percent, compared with 54 percent for South Asia and 65 percent for East Asia and the Pacific. Levels of enrollment differed substantially among African countries, with attendance as low as 17.1 percent in Niger, compared with 77 percent in South Africa. The adult literacy rate in Africa is also low, though at 63.2 percent in 2002 it was slightly higher than the 57.6 percent recorded in South Asia. Perhaps more significantly, it was well below East Asia's 90.3 percent.

QUANTITY AND QUALITY OF EDUCATION: BOTH MATTER

Although still inadequate, African countries have made progress in increasing the number of their citizens going through school. At the time of political independence, only a tiny percentage of privileged people received any type of formal education. Today schools can be found even in remote villages. However, some economists have questioned the emphasis placed by governments and international development agencies on enrollment. What is crucial for generating economic growth, they say, is the quality of education, not merely the quantity. Quality is defined by measured mathematical and science skills and knowledge that enhances the individual's technological capabilities.

In this respect, the quality of education in most African countries is very poor. This partly reflects the fact that the small amounts of public funds invested in education have to be spread thinly in order to provide schooling to large numbers of people. As a result, most African schools, from primary to post-secondary, make do with very basic infrastructure and lack science equipment. Public spending on education as a percentage of total government expenditures is not particularly low in

Africa when compared with levels in other regions of the world, but the absolute sums spent on schools are trivial because of the low income.

Africa's poor educational quality also reflects the pattern of its governments' budgets, which disproportionately expend more on secondary schooling than on primary schooling. East Asian countries' education spending made greater impact on human capital development because these countries channeled more funds to primary education and focused more on mathematics and science.

Today sub-Saharan Africa has an average primary school completion rate of just 59 percent. According to the World Bank, on current trends the region will not achieve universal primary education until 2061, much later than the UN Millennium

A teacher instructs his students in a newly rehabilitated secondary school in Sierra Leone. During the country's civil war from 1991 to 2002, warring parties destroyed many schools as part of their terror campaigns.

Development Goals' 2015 target. However, some African countries, such as Ghana, Kenya, Nigeria, and Tanzania, can reach the 2015 goal if they maintain recent progress.

Although Asian governments gave greater weight to primary schools in their education budgets, their countries nevertheless were able to build large pools of higher education graduates, especially in the sciences and technology. Africa has produced relatively few university graduates. According to UNESCO (the United Nations Educational, Scientific and Cultural Organization), South Africa was the only country in sub-Saharan Africa that had more than 1,000 university students per 100,000 people in 1996. Perhaps more telling is a comparison between African countries and high-performance East Asian nations in their stock of scientists and engineers. For instance, while the number of natural science university students in Ethiopia grew from 106 in 1960 to 1,730 in 1996, the number of such students in the Republic of Korea rose from 8,802 to 100,120 over the same period. Similarly, while the number of engineering students in Nigeria rose from only 28 in 1960 to 22,080 in 1996, in Indonesia the number increased from 3,245 to 293,946. And Africa continues to lag behind in providing its people with opportunities for advanced education. In sub-Saharan Africa in 2001, according to UNESCO statistics, enrollment in postsecondary education totaled just 2.5 percent of the university-age population. This was more than five times lower than the enrollment ratio for East Asia/Oceania and more than nine times lower than the world total.

A major problem facing African countries in raising the quantity and quality of education is their gross lack of funding. Even when governments dedicate a large proportion of their public spending to education, the absolute amounts expended remain paltry. Between 2000 and 2002, public spending on education as a percentage of total government outlays was above 20

A South African student conducts a chemistry experiment with a science kit. Among the many critical issues facing Africa's underfunded educational systems is the need to produce more graduates with scientific and technical training. The dearth of scientists and engineers stifles economic growth in many African countries.

percent in at least seven African countries. But such high rates did not translate into much in dollar terms because overall state revenues were so low.

No doubt many African governments could make better use of available resources by reducing corruption, eliminating waste, and assigning priorities more rationally. Nevertheless, even with good governance, poor nations would be unable to fund the production of quality human capital because of the lack of economic growth. The problem is cyclical.

POOR HEALTH UNDERMINES ECONOMIC GROWTH

As with education, investment in health care in Africa has been grossly inadequate. In 2003 health expenditures averaged only

$13 per citizen in sub-Saharan Africa (excluding South Africa) and were as low as $10 per citizen in 16 countries. Contrast these levels with conditions in the developed world, where health spending is more than $2,000 per person.

One of the obvious results of the low investment in health care is that millions of Africans suffer or die from preventable or curable ailments. Over the last three decades, life expectancy in sub-Saharan Africa has risen only marginally, from 45.2 years in the first half of the 1970s to 46.1 years in 2000–2005, according to the United Nations. This deplorable state of affairs contrasts with big gains in life expectancy made in other regions of the world. For instance, in East Asia during the past three decades, the average lifespan has risen from 60.5 years to 69.9 years, fast approaching the 78.4 years in high-income advanced countries.

In many African countries life expectancy has fallen dramatically. For example, in Botswana it has dropped from 56 years to slightly more than 36 years over the past three decades. In eight other African countries, life expectancy has also dipped below 40 years. The major reason for this is the HIV/AIDS epidemic, which has claimed millions of Africans and threatens to take many more. The United Nations agency UNAIDS predicts that Africa will suffer 55 million deaths attributable to AIDS between 2000 and 2015. Sub-Saharan Africa is by far the worst affected region, home to nearly two-thirds of all people with HIV/AIDS. The average HIV adult infection rate in the region is 7.7 percent. (In calculating HIV infection rates, adults are defined as all people between the ages of 15 and 49.) In many countries in eastern and southern Africa, infection rates are incredibly high—almost 40 percent in Botswana and Swaziland and above 20 percent in Lesotho, South Africa, and Zimbabwe. Although Nigeria's infection rate is much lower, at an estimated 5.4 percent, the impact of the disease will likely be magnified by the West African country's large population.

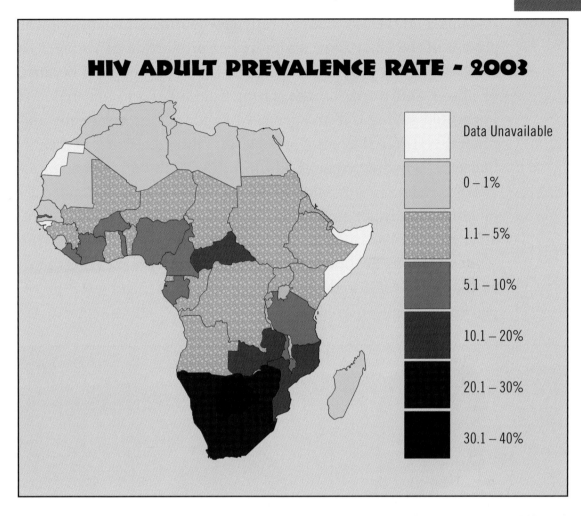

HIV ADULT PREVALENCE RATE - 2003

Data Unavailable

0 – 1%

1.1 – 5%

5.1 – 10%

10.1 – 20%

20.1 – 30%

30.1 – 40%

HIV/AIDS has decimated sub-Saharan Africa. Since the beginning of the epidemic in the early 1980s, the disease has claimed more than 15 million lives in the region, including an estimated 2.4 million in 2005 alone. With only about 10 percent of the world's population, sub-Saharan Africa is home to more than 60 percent of the people infected with HIV. The epidemic has had disastrous economic consequences, depriving African nations of large numbers of workers, lowering productivity, and consuming government resources that could have been devoted to development.

Besides the human misery caused by the HIV/AIDS epidemic—some 11 million African children have been orphaned by it—the disease has undermined growth in human capital in Africa. The impact may, in some respects, be comparable with the devastation of the slave trade 200 years ago. Like the slave trade, HIV/AIDS is devouring people in their most productive years, while fueling a climate of uncertainty and fear among survivors.

Its impact on the economies of affected countries includes slower growth of the labor force and a higher proportion of young, less skilled, and less productive workers; lower productivity because of illness and worry on the job or time off work; and reduced household saving due to increased expenses for treatment and funerals. HIV/AIDS also eats deeply into government health budgets. Providing expensive antiretroviral-therapy drugs to all AIDS sufferers in sub-Saharan Africa would cost an estimated $9 billion annually, an amount far beyond the meager means of the affected nations. In its 2003 Economic Report on Africa, the United Nations Economic Commission for Africa (ECA) estimated that HIV/AIDS reduces GDP growth in Africa by 0.5 to 2.6 percent per year on average.

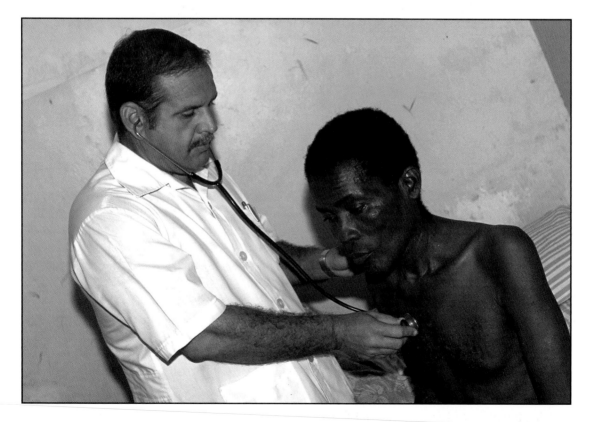

A doctor in Ghana treats a patient with tuberculosis. Patients with a new, resistant strain of TB are prescribed four drugs (isoniazid, rifampin, pyrazinamides, and ethambutol or streptomycin); however, the annual cost of the drugs can be as high as $1,000, far more than the average African can afford.

Other costly diseases undermining economic development in Africa include malaria and tuberculosis. Malaria kills almost 1 million Africans per year, a number that represents about 90 percent of the fatal cases of the disease worldwide. Africa's GDP would be as much as $100 billion greater if malaria had been eliminated years ago, according to estimates cited in the ECA report. And in countries badly affected by tuberculosis, the loss of productivity due to the disease is estimated at 4 to 7 percent of GDP.

Poor health is a major impediment to agricultural growth in Africa. People who are sick are unable to work the fields. Scientists have warned that farming in parts of Africa has declined at an alarming rate since the start of the AIDS epidemic. The virus is ravaging agriculture; the area of cultivated land has dropped by as much as 68 percent in parts of Kenya, for example.

THE BRAIN DRAIN: GAINS AND LOSSES

African leaders contend that their nations' meager stocks of human capital have been depleted by the so-called brain drain—the migration of skilled and highly educated individuals from poorer to richer places. They say the brain drain is depriving the region of much-needed human capital, making it difficult to reduce poverty. Over the years many thousands of qualified professionals, such as doctors, nurses, engineers, and academics, have left African countries to work abroad, mainly in Europe and America. According to the 2005 report of the Commission for Africa, the continent loses an average of 70,000 skilled personnel a year to developed countries. Zambia, the report said, has lost all but 400 of its 1,600 doctors. And according to the World Bank's Global Monitoring Report on the Millennium Development Goals, there may be more Nigerian doctors in New

York than in Nigeria and more Malawian doctors in Manchester, England, than in Malawi. About 60 percent of graduates from Ghana Medical School between 1986 and 1995 left the West African country, with more than half heading for the United Kingdom.

Anti-poverty groups blame the exodus of educated people for the poor standards of public services, especially health care, in the countries they leave. It is also said that when workers migrate, the investment made in their upbringing and education is lost to the recipient countries. The cost to Africa has been put as high as $4 billion per year.

Nevertheless, the economic consequences of the movement of skilled labor out of Africa are not as straightforward as are the economic consequences of the loss of workers through disease. The idea that Africa is short of human capital because of brain drain is debatable. African countries continue to lack sufficient qualified professionals in employment because their public and private institutions lack the funds to pay for these professionals' services. Bearing in mind that demand is both the desire and ability to purchase an item or service, most African countries have insufficient domestic demand for the types of labor that have been migrating. For instance, hospitals in Kenya are short of medical staff not so much because Kenyan doctors and nurses have chosen to work abroad, but because the country's medical authorities lack the funds to employ more staff.

Educated Africans leave their homelands for greener pastures abroad mainly because of the lack of appropriate employment opportunities at home. The movement of labor from poor to rich countries, rather than being viewed as an entirely detrimental flow of resources, could be seen as providing an outlet for excess workers. Furthermore, labor migration may contribute to the building of human capital in Africa by enabling countries to train and educate more people than they can immediately utilize.

It can also enhance their stock of human capital, as skilled workers who temporarily move abroad may return to their country of origin with more knowledge and experience than they possessed when they left.

Lack of employment opportunities in Africa is a disincentive to investment in human capital. Generally, people invest their time, effort, and money in acquiring skills and knowledge because they hope to gain from the use of the acquired capabilities. If getting an education is unlikely to help an individual gain the rewards he or she desires, then that individual may well choose other options. This applies not only to higher education, but also to lower-level schooling. In some parts of Africa truancy in primary schools is high because pupils and their parents do not see the point of attendance when the experience will not further their chances of escaping poverty. High returns to education, whether through employment at home or abroad, can be a strong incentive, encouraging households to invest in the education of their children.

Emigration abroad by talented Africans is not all a losing proposition. Remittances from nationals working abroad have become a major source of external development finance for many developing countries. Workers' remittances to sub-Saharan Africa total about $4 billion a year. Unlike foreign aid, which can be captured by corrupt governments, remittances from abroad go directly to individuals, many of whom are poor.

POPULATION GROWTH AND DEVELOPMENT

Despite Africa's loss of people due to disease and migration, the continent's population has grown rapidly, with implications for its economic development. Sub-Saharan Africa has experienced a phenomenal increase in the number of its inhabitants since the colonial period. According to estimates by the economic historian Angus Maddison in his widely acclaimed book *The World Economy: A Millennial Perspective*, sub-Saharan Africa's population increased more than 10-fold between 1820 and 2001, from 63.25 million to 672 million—with the biggest growth taking place in the 20th century.

Some analysts believe that this sharp rise in population was detrimental to economic growth in Africa. They point out that the growth in the number of humans was not matched by growth in infrastructure and output of goods, thereby leading to increased scarcity. This, in turn, fueled social and ethnic conflicts between competing groups, especially where shortages of water and arable land existed.

In its World Development Report 1984, the World Bank expressed concern that rapid population growth was undermining economic growth in some developing countries. The report said that population growth at a rate above 2 percent acts as a brake on development. Sub-Saharan Africa's population has been growing at about 2.7 percent since the 1970s, though the rate is expected to slow down to 2.1 percent between 2002 and 2015.

Poverty fuels high birthrates, and rapid population growth leads to more poverty. Breaking the cycle will be difficult for Africa, whose population is projected to nearly triple in the 21st century.

The World Bank noted that in most countries in sub-Saharan Africa economic activity slowed in the 1970s while population continued to grow rapidly, resulting in stagnating or declining per capita income. Countries with high population, propelled by high fertility, can find themselves caught in a vicious circle whereby the slow pace at which development reaches the poor contributes to rapid population growth, making the elimination of poverty increasingly difficult. (Parents in poor countries, especially in rural areas, tend to have large families for several reasons, including the likelihood that some of their children will die in infancy or early childhood, the need for extra labor to work the land, and the desire to ensure that they will be taken care of in old age, which is an especially important consideration in nations that lack social security programs.)

The economic consequences of rapid population expansion are numerous. Poor families tend to have few savings. Parents have less to invest in the education of their children. Increased demand for public services results in investment being spread overly thin. The World Bank concluded that slowing population growth is a difficult challenge, but one that needs to be addressed.

Although rapid population growth has been cited as a major impediment to economic development, it is necessary to have populated urban centers within a country. Without major cities needing roads, sewage, and waterworks, there is little incentive to invest in the infrastructure necessary for greater economic growth. Higher population density creates jobs because it requires workers to maintain roads and pipelines and provide services. In spite of the huge increase in Africa's population over the past two centuries, the continent's population density remains comparatively low. Only 7 of sub-Saharan Africa's 48 countries have more than 30 million people, and just 4 have more than 40 million people.

Having small populations can be favorable for oil-endowed countries such as Equatorial Guinea and Sao Tome and Principe, but for nations with huge land space and few natural resources, like Mali, Niger, and Chad, sparseness poses enormous challenges for development.

If long-term projections prove accurate, Africa will experience the greatest increase in population among all the world's regions. In a report published in 2004, the United Nations Population Division indicated that the number of inhabitants in the entire African continent, including North Africa, could jump from 796 million in 2000 to 2.25 billion in 2100, before dropping to 2.1 billion in 2300. Under this scenario, Africa's share of world population would go from 13.1 percent in 2000 to 24.9 percent in 2100 and 24.2 percent in 2300.

# STRUCTURAL IMPEDIMENTS TO WEALTH CREATION

Most African countries have remained highly dependent on the production of primary commodities, while fast-growth countries in other developing regions have managed to diversify their economies. Traditional agricultural crops such as coffee, cotton, and sugar currently account for half of Africa's total agricultural exports. On average, African countries derive over 21 percent of their GDP from primary products, compared with about 10 percent for other developing nations and less than 3 percent for developed nations. With this level of dependence, African economies have been vulnerable to rapid changes in market conditions for these commodities.

DECLINE OF AGRICULTURE

Over the last 140 years, real world commodity prices (prices adjusted for inflation) have been falling by about 1 percent per year. But perhaps more importantly, there has been increased volatility in prices since the early 1970s, sending confusing signals to African cultivators.

According to the World Bank, Africa's share of world trade dropped from around 6 percent in 1980 to 2 percent in 2002—less than its estimated 3.7 percent share in 1913, during colonial rule. More specifically, Africa's share of world agricultural exports plummeted from 8.6 percent in 1961 to 3 percent in 1996. The decline stemmed not only from the fall in world commodity prices and the limited composition of Africa's exports, but also from the loss of market share to other, more dynamic regions producing many of Africa's traditional commodities. For example, Malaysia, whose per capita income in 1960 was less than that of Nigeria, had, by the 1990s, grown to be 10 times richer than the African giant, largely through the export of cash crops for which Nigeria was once world leader. After taking palm oil seedlings from Nigeria in the 1960s, Malaysia rose to become the world's principal producer and exporter of the commodity, while Nigeria's exports shriveled to insignificance. Because of the emergence of major new commodity producers in Asia and Latin America, as well as increases in productivity, global commodity supplies grew more rapidly than demand, consequently pushing prices down.

Africa also lost its market share in world agricultural exports because its farmers did not diversify their output. Although real prices for agricultural commodities have declined over the past 40 years, the rate of decline has varied from commodity to commodity. Raw materials, tropical beverages, oil crops, and cereals—which Africa mostly depends on—have experienced the sharpest falls, while horticultural products, meat, and dairy goods have not been as badly hit. According to the Food and Agriculture Organization (FAO), developing countries (other than the least developed) have more than doubled the proportion of horticultural, meat, and dairy products in their overall agricultural exports.

At the same time, they have reduced their dependence on tropical beverages and raw materials. In the 1960s tropical beverages and raw materials made up 55 percent of their agricultural exports; by 2001 these commodities accounted for only about 30 percent of agricultural exports. Among the least developed countries, however, dependence on tropical beverages and raw materials for export earnings has risen: these commodities accounted for 59 percent of agricultural exports in the 1960s, and 72 percent in 2001, according to the FAO.

There are a number of possible explanations for Africa's failure to use its colonial legacy of strong agricultural production as a base for sustainable economic development. The political elites in power at the time of independence tended to be urban centric, viewing social and economic progress in terms of creating modern physical structures in cities and pursuing models of industrialization that were detached from their country's agrarian roots. They maintained the dual economy created by the colonial powers, whereby a modern sector linked to the global economy existed separately from (and almost as an enclave within) the traditional, subsistence-based sector. But whereas the colonial approach to development facilitated the extraction of primary products for external markets and neglected the internal market, Africa's black rulers emphasized the internal urban market and neglected agriculture.

Small-scale farmers, who account for the bulk of Africa's agricultural output, received relatively little in the way of development resources. Government budgets clearly favored the cities and urban elites. When African governments did increase budget support for agricultural sectors, much of the investment went into state farms, big irrigation schemes, and other capital-intensive activities. Most of these projects, often supported by external development loans, had little impact on output. In some cases the amount of money African governments spent on agriculture was

Women and children pick green beans at the Dodicha Vegetable Cooperative in Ethiopia. As is the case with other impoverished African countries, Ethiopia relies heavily on agriculture, which employs an estimated 80 percent of the workforce.

not insignificant. For instance, during the 1979–1983 civilian government in Nigeria, more than $2 billion was spent on large-scale irrigation projects, yet gains in agricultural output were negligible. Money was lavished on government agencies, which were supposed to bring about a "green revolution" that would turn Africa's most populous nation into a food basket within a few years. Instead, these state agencies became notorious for funneling public funds into private pockets. The dismal results of government agricultural schemes in Africa contrast with more successful state initiatives in Asia, especially India, where between the mid-1960s and the late 1970s agricultural output was significantly boosted through the "green revolution." India's effort included the expansion of farming areas, the building of irrigation facilities, and the development of high-yield seeds.

A significant portion of government spending on rural development in Africa has gone into relatively disfavored, poorer regions with low and varying rainfall. This was partly motivated by the desire for regional balance and poverty reduction in countries marked by uneven development. Though laudable in terms of achieving social equality, it meant that public investments to boost agricultural output could not achieve the maximum yields possible. Projects in low-yielding environments did not add much to output, whereas the more potentially fertile and high-yielding regions continued to underperform due to inadequate investment.

The incentive structure in most African countries did not encourage farmers to expand output. Prices paid to growers were often far too low to enable them to invest in better tools and

The Nigerian government commissioned a 23-mile canal to bring water from Lake Chad to farms for irrigation. However, drought caused the lake to recede, so the canal never carried water to the fields, wasting millions of dollars.

ingredients. In many countries, farmers were compelled to sell their produce to agents of price-fixing marketing boards run by the government. The boards were established during the colonial era to stabilize producer prices, promote the economic development of the producing industries, and finance research. Initially, many of the boards used their price-setting powers to bring about improvements in the quality of export crops. But the system was abused as African politicians sought to capture the funds raised by the boards to enrich themselves or finance non-agricultural projects. The gap between domestic prices and international prices grew, amounting to an additional tax on farmers. Even though governments provided farmers with subsidized production inputs, such as fertilizers and seeds, the more efficient growers would have been significantly better off had they been allowed to receive international prices for their crops and used their profits to invest in expanding their output. Marketing boards were scrapped in many African countries in the late 1980s as part of economic liberalization reforms.

One of the factors in the interrelated problem of rural poverty and poor agricultural performance is that most farmers operate plots of land that are too small to justify major investment in upgrading their production level. This is partly due to the persistence of farming systems based on customary land tenure. Under this system, property rights are ostensibly controlled and allocated according to traditional practices, which are distinct from the Western concepts of private land ownership, including the right to sell one's holdings. Under the traditional system, land belongs to the family and the community. It is an entitlement of members of the community but cannot be sold, at least not to outsiders. Although this system ensures that most people in the community have access to land, it also means that individual farms are small and become smaller with growth in the population.

Even when farmers own the field they till, they often do not possess formal legal ownership. This is because in most parts of Africa title deeds to land were never issued, and the process of registering property can be lengthy and costly, especially for the poor. Similarly, poor people in urban shantytowns often do not possess the formal documentation that would give them property rights with regard to their dwellings.

When people lack formal ownership of their belongings, they are denied the property rights that were crucial to economic development in the industrialized nations. For instance, they are unable to use their land as collateral to obtain bank loans—and without such loans, they cannot invest in enhancing their productive capacity. Nor can they easily sell their assets. In 1997 Hernando de Soto, a Peruvian economist, estimated the total value of dwellings owned informally by Africans at $580 billion, and the total value of land cultivated but not formally owned by African farmers at $390 billion. The sum of these two figures amounts to almost $1 trillion—nearly twice Africa's entire GDP.

Private property rights are not only important in enabling people to use their assets to raise capital, they are crucial in giving owners confidence to use their economic resources to create further wealth. Private property rights also allow inefficient farmers to sell their holdings to more efficient producers, facilitating the enlargement of farms for greater productivity.

African governments have embarked on land reforms to establish market-oriented

Preparing to till a field, Uganda. When a family only farms a small plot of land, as is typical in Africa, spending money on more efficient tools would be a waste, since there is no chance of producing enough surplus to recoup the cost.

access to land to give owners private entitlement backed by legal rights. But progress has been slow due to the sensitive nature of land ownership and distribution in a continent where some 70 percent of the population lives in rural areas. Many people oppose the privatization of land, contending that land belongs to the community and that social relations within and between local communities in Africa have traditionally been able to provide secure land rights. Such voices are particularly strong in ex-settler colonies, such as South Africa and Zimbabwe, where small numbers of white farmers gained disproportionately high amounts of the countries' fertile lands based on private entitlements obtained through conquest.

The difficult question facing African policy makers is whether to view land primarily as a means of production or as an object of wealth redistribution. The experience of more developed economies indicates that the move from subsistence farming to commercial cultivation involves some enlargement of farm sizes and the development of farming as a business conducted by a tiny percentage of the population. Millions of Africans depend on working the land for their livelihood, making it difficult for governments to push for liberalization reforms, which would invariably result in many inefficient producers being forced to abandon their land so efficient workers could boost production.

GENETICALLY MODIFIED FOOD AND FOOD PRODUCTION

A possible solution to Africa's agricultural predicament is the use of genetically modified (GM) crops. But African countries have been reluctant to import GM food or invest in biotechnology because they fear losing export markets in Europe if their crops become contaminated with GM seeds. There are also concerns about the safety of GM food for human consumption and the environment. Worldwide, the agricultural area given over to GM crops has grown 47-fold since 1996, but developing nations have remained largely hesitant to use such crops. In Africa, only South Africa grows GM crops to any significant extent. A number of African countries have banned the importation of GM products. In 2002 Zambia declined a U.S. offer of corn because some of it contained GM products.

Proponents of the use of GM food and technology contend that for a continent with nearly half its population undernourished or underfed, the deployment of science to solve the crisis should be an obvious option. Agro-biotechnology, farming based on genetically modified organisms, may allow higher yields, improve farmers' profits, ease domestic food shortages, and facilitate the production of new, quality products with potential for increasing export earnings. Also critical is that the introduction of GM crops in Africa may actually benefit the environment. For instance, some crops can be modified to be resistant to pests, removing the need to spray with pesticides. The technology also holds the possibility of developing varieties that can flourish in arid conditions. Supporters of GM food dismiss the health

Opponents of genetically modified foods protest outside the San Diego Convention Center at the start of BIO 2001, a biotechnology-industry conference. African governments have resisted the use of GM crops and have barred the importation of GM foods, even when facing a humanitarian crisis. Zambia, for example, declined a gift of corn from the United States during a 2002 famine because of fears that the corn contained some GM kernels.

concerns of critics, pointing to the fact that people in the United States have been eating GM crops for years without any known side effects.

However, opponents of bioengineering say it remains unproven technology. There is also concern among many Africans that the adoption of GM technology could make their countries more vulnerable to profiteering Western suppliers and even more dependent on advanced nations (which could restrict developing countries' access to the seeds). Yet the most important concern is probably that adoption of GM technology would hamper African countries' trade prospects with Europe, where consumers remain skeptical about bioengineered products.

THE CURSE OF MINERAL RESOURCE WEALTH

African countries that have been dependent on high-value natural resources, such as minerals and crude oil, have not fared better than those reliant on agricultural commodities. Indeed, for many African countries a rich resource endowment has seemed more of a curse than a blessing. High-value natural resources generate what economists call rent—payment to a factor of production in excess of the amount necessary to keep it employed in its current use. For instance, if the least an oil producer would accept is $2 per barrel, because this price covers the production cost and leaves the producer with sufficient profit, but the market price for oil rises to $50 per barrel, the difference of $48 is "rent." Windfall revenues from high-rent resources encourage politicians and others to extract some of the surplus income for themselves. This "rent seeking" has fueled rampant corruption and created conflicts between political groups battling for access to the wealth. It has been one of the main underlying causes of civil war and secession bids in post-colonial Africa. Natural resource wealth finances rebel groups and encourages the local population to support secession wars, as has happened in such places as Biafra in Nigeria, Cabinda in Angola, and Katanga in the Congo. Many of the internal conflicts still raging in African countries stem from disputes over control of natural resources. For example, gold deposits in the northeastern part of the Democratic Republic of the Congo have been the catalyst for much conflict in that section of the country.

Wealth in natural resources has also made countries susceptible to what has been called the "Dutch disease." This is when the discovery of natural resources leads to significant increases in capital inflow, with the result that the value of the national currency appreciates, making non-resource exports less competitive.

Sierra Leone's 1991–2002 civil war was fought, in large part, for control of the country's rich diamond mines. In turn, sales of the gemstones—dubbed "blood diamonds"—financed the weapons purchases of rebel factions, including the notorious Revolutionary United Front (RUF). The RUF carried on a brutal campaign of terror, amputating the arms, legs, ears, or lips of tens of thousands of civilians.

Resource-rich countries have been prone to large, sudden, and unexpected changes in world output prices, especially in the case of oil. The tendency has been for governments to substantially raise their expenditure levels during boom periods and then find themselves plunged into financial crisis when prices contract. Large, unexpected earnings from natural resources have had mesmerizing effects on governments, fueling the illusion of national wealth and weakening incentives to develop a broad tax base.

Natural resource wealth need not be a curse. Some African countries have been able to capitalize on their resource endowment without succumbing to greed and euphoric shortsightedness. For instance, while diamond riches brought social catastrophe and civil war to Sierra Leone, diamonds proved critical to the economic success of Botswana. Relatively strong institutions promoting good governance have enabled Botswana to avoid the pitfalls of resource wealth. The political influence of Botswanan cattle-exporting groups also ensured that rising diamond production did not lead to an overvalued exchange rate and the "Dutch disease." The government makes budgetary provision to ensure that mineral revenues are invested in schooling, health care, and infrastructure rather than consumed through frivolous government expenditures.

THE FAILURE OF MANUFACTURING

With few exceptions, modern manufacturing production has not taken firm root in Africa. This is unfortunate, as the growth of manufacturing is a prerequisite for rapid and sustainable poverty reduction because it offers the greatest opportunity for new employment generation. Manufacturing has been in decline in Africa for two decades. Its contribution to the continent's GDP has dropped from 17 percent in 1990 to 14 percent in 2003.

However, the distribution of manufacturing activity in the continent is uneven. South Africa accounts for more than a quarter of sub-Saharan Africa's manufacturing value added (MVA)—the measure of the additional value created at the manufacturing stage of production. Only 10 countries in the region have an MVA of $1 billion or more. With the exception of South Africa and Mauritius, MVA per capita in sub-Saharan Africa is very low: 40 of the region's 48 economies have an MVA per capita below $250. In 33 countries, manufacturing accounts for less than 12.5 percent of GDP. The countries that have achieved the highest manufacturing activity per capita have been ones with small populations. Seven of the top eight—the exception being South Africa—have populations of less than 2 million.

In addition to the factors highlighted above, the underdevelopment of manufacturing in Africa is attributable largely to the continent's small internal markets, failure to enter export markets, and low technological capabilities. The ability of a firm to expand its operation depends to a large degree on the size of its market. For instance, a furniture maker operating in an economy with only 100 potential customers would have no reason to invest in new machinery or employ higher-skilled managers to be able to meet the demand of 1,000 consumers. Doing so would mean incurring additional costs without the prospect of recouping the investment.

However, if the size of the market were to increase to 1,000 or more, such an investment would be wise because the firm would be able not only to raise its output but also to reduce unit cost of production through improved efficiency. The division of labor—the breakdown of labor into specialized functions involved in the production process—is limited by the size of the market. In a small market, people and firms cannot specialize to the same extent they can in larger markets, which can absorb the increased production resulting from the more efficient production arrangement.

Firms serving small markets are not able to exploit economies of scale, and thus they produce at high costs. This means that firms in a small economy are effectively precluded from producing certain types of products for which unit costs fall significantly when they are produced on a large scale. For instance, it would make little sense to set up a motor vehicle manufacturing company in an economy with demand for only 100 cars a year. The unit cost of producing such a low volume of vehicles would be much more than the cost of importing the same number of vehicles. This is one of the reasons why small economies face limited opportunities to diversify.

Workers in this factory—one of several hundred South African plants that manufacture automobile components—are assembling vinyl accessories. South Africa is among only a handful of sub-Saharan African countries with thriving export sectors.

LIMITATIONS OF PRODUCING FOR SMALL MARKETS

Africa has many microstates and small states. Eleven of its nations have less than 1.5 million people, and 21 have populations of less than 5 million. Only seven states have populations of more than 30 million. Even African countries with large populations have economies with very small markets—bearing in mind that consumer demand entails not only people's desire for a good or service but also their ability to pay for it. Although Nigeria is the ninth most populous country in the world, with some 131 million people, the size of the

Nigerian economy is less than that of Norway, which has a population of less than 5 million but a per capita income of nearly $38,000. Adjusted for purchasing power parity, Nigeria has a per capita income of only $900.

Producers in countries with small populations and domestic markets can expand their economic opportunities by pursuing export markets. This is why small economies have tended to be more open to foreign trade than larger ones. All poor-nation economies have relatively small domestic markets. Those that have achieved rapid industrialization have done so by building up their export sectors. Not even China—despite its mammoth population—could have raised its industrial production to the levels seen during the past two decades without turning to export markets.

Unfortunately, African countries—with the exceptions of Mauritius, South Africa, and Lesotho—have not broken into export markets in a big way. Most remain much less open to trade than economically successful small states in other regions of the world. Many African countries have industries producing basic necessities for domestic markets, such as textiles, garments, leather goods, food, and beverages. They generally operate at low levels of output, making just enough profit to stay in business. Over the last two decades, however, they have faced increasing competition at the hands of cheap imports from more efficient, larger-scale producers in other regions of the world, especially Asia.

African producers encounter many problems that make their workers less productive than workers in other regions that also have low labor costs. Labor productivity (the amount of output from a unit of labor input) in Africa lags substantially behind labor productivity in East Asia, for example. In other words, Asia's more dynamic economies obtain a greater amount of goods or services per hour of labor employed than do most

Large numbers of Africans earn their livelihood in the informal sector of the economy. Pictured here: textile vendors in a Rwandan street market.

African economies. Labor productivity involves more than personal effort. In fact, throughout much of Africa, low labor productivity is mainly the consequence of problems unrelated to employee performance. Non-labor costs in Africa are significantly higher than in advancing Asia. One of the major causes of low African output is the appalling state of infrastructure services, such as electricity supplies, transport, and customs. A worker operating under conditions where power and water supplies are unreliable will understandably produce less because much of his or her time is spent idling through power cuts. Working with old and poorly maintained equipment also affects output, as does operating under incompetent managers. Labor productivity in Africa also lags behind that in many Asian countries because in Africa the actual cost of employing workers in the formal sector is often higher. Even though overall income per person is lower in Africa—in part because so many people work in the kinds of small household enterprises and "off-the-books" jobs that make up the informal sector—in some African countries formal sector wages are considerably above the national minimum wage and are higher than wages in Asian countries with low labor costs, such as China. This means that, all other things being equal, one dollar's worth of labor will yield more output in Asia than in Africa.

African producers find themselves at a substantial disadvantage in competition against foreign producers who operate at higher scales of production and lower unit costs. African governments have responded to their predicament by maintaining high import tariffs and non-tariff barriers to protect local industries. But these protectionist policies have done little to boost domestic production. Trade barriers have encouraged smuggling, which deprives the government of tax revenue while failing to protect local industries against competition. When protectionist measures are effective, inefficient local businesses lack the incentive to invest in measures to raise productivity, such as capital improvement and increased efficiency. Perhaps most importantly, high-cost production for a captured domestic market offers local producers few opportunities to expand their capacity because of the small size of the market. Under these circumstances, the main demand stimulus to industrial growth will come from population growth rather than rising income, as happens in more dynamic and open economies.

ON THE MARGINS OF THE GLOBAL MARKET

Unfortunately, African countries have not undergone the fundamental shift in strategy for industrialization that has occurred in many countries in East Asia, where economic emphasis has moved from trying to satisfy domestic demand to responding to global demand (which of course includes local consumers). Asian producers have established a wide range of industries producing goods, finished and intermediary, for which demand exists anywhere in the world, even if there are currently few consumers in their own countries. This export orientation has greatly broadened their scope of operations and enabled them to achieve the benefits of the division of labor and large-scale production. By diversifying the industrial sector and producing for much deeper markets, export-oriented developing countries have been able to create millions of new jobs at home, thereby increasing local incomes and boosting domestic demand.

Africa has not had much success in linking to the global production chain—the network resulting from the international division of labor—beyond being the supplier of primary products. Most finished consumer goods are the culmination of numerous production processes that take place across many countries. For instance, dozens of firms operating in different parts of the world produce the components that go into the manufacturing of a shirt. First, there are the makers of the various machines and intermediate products used in the textile and garment industries. Then there is the process of manufacturing the shirt, which is quite complex and involves different firms that are responsible for different parts of the garment. Improvements in transportation and communications have allowed the production chain to be further broken up into more components. At every stage in the production process, producers add value, for which they are rewarded. In this continuum from the production of the raw material through the processing of the finished product, the level of reward tends to increase as firms move into more sophisticated production activities involving greater human skill and use of higher technology. Africa's predicament has been its inability to move much beyond the first and most elementary stage of the production chain—the supply of primary commodities. Diversification up the production chain would make African economies less susceptible to fluctuations in commodity prices.

Even in the sale of primary products, most African countries are quite limited in their range of exports. Ten of sub-Saharan Africa's 48 countries relied on a single product for more than 75 percent of their exports in 2002. This group included Botswana, for which diamonds accounted for nearly 90 percent of export earnings. Only South Africa had a diversified export base, with 60 products accounting for more than 70 percent of its exports in 2002.

Failure to move up the production chain and diversify exports has been due largely to low levels of skill and technological know-how as well as inadequate infrastructure in the continent. Africa has also lost out in this globalization process because it has not attracted investors with the requisite capital and market knowledge to help it shift gears. Much of the dynamic export-oriented manufacturing activities in fast-growth Asian countries like China have stemmed from foreign investment. For instance, foreign firms are estimated to account for about half of China's industrial exports and as much as 85 percent of its high-technology sales.

INADEQUATE INFRASTRUCTURE

Africa is grossly deficient in all kinds of infrastructure essential for economic development and growth. In some parts of Africa, farmers lose as much as half of their produce for lack of adequate post-harvest storage. Throughout the region, women and girls trek an average of four miles (6.4 kilometers) a day to collect water, making their daily productivity low. The lack of farm-to-market roads restricts the supply capacity of farmers.

Poor infrastructure is a major obstacle to the upgrading of African economies from primary-product to intermediate- and high-technology output. Inadequate and unreliable electricity supplies make it extremely difficult for modern industrial companies to function competitively. Sub-Saharan Africa has the lowest electricity production of all regions, and in 2000 only a quarter of its inhabitants had access to power. Firms incur huge costs installing and running private electricity-generating plants to back up or substitute for supplies from the national grid.

Poor communications also place African producers at a disadvantage, as does inadequate transport. In Uganda, transport costs add the equivalent of an 80 percent tax on clothing exports. It costs more than twice as much to transport a container from

Kampala to the coast as it costs to ship the container from the coast to Los Angeles.

Lack of infrastructure not only stands as a serious barrier to the growth of enterprises able to compete in international markets, but also prevents global production networks from establishing facilities in Africa. Many African countries have tried to overcome this problem by setting up export production zones as a way of providing suitable industrial infrastructure for export-oriented activity. By concentrating facilities in a relatively small area, it is possible to economize and ensure the delivery of good-quality services. Yet this strategy has invariably left domestic producers at a disadvantage.

Substantial sums of money have been invested in infrastructure development since the African countries gained independence, but with little impact on economic growth. Between 1990 and 2002, infrastructure investment in sub-Saharan Africa totaled some $150 billion, all but $27.8 billion of this coming from the public sector. Poor management, corruption, and shoddy maintenance of facilities have been largely to blame for substandard performance.

Even where governments have been relatively honest and well intentioned, facilitating economic growth has often not been their primary motivation. In ethnically diverse nations, governments have endeavored to spread the provision of infrastructure services across competing regions. Indeed, governments have sought to establish new industries in underdeveloped areas and then develop the infrastructure to service them. Although this approach to development may be morally just and pragmatic in geopolitical terms, it has typically meant that infrastructure is underdeveloped in areas where private industry is most concentrated.

Government decisions to relocate the national political capital from the commercial center of the country—as happened in

Cameroon, the Republic of the Congo, Ivory Coast, Nigeria, and Tanzania—have led to huge infrastructure investment in places that are remote from the centers of economic activity. Governments have also endeavored to boost public services in marginalized areas, sometimes to calm political and social unrest in volatile regions. For instance, Nigeria's federal government has increased development funding in the oil-rich Niger Delta in response to growing violence in the impoverished region. Though such investment may be politically expedient, as it helps secure the safety of oil installations, it has not had as much impact on increasing national economic growth as would improvement of utilities in the country's industrial centers.

An executive of a South African electricity-supplies company. South Africa is one of the few sub-Saharan African countries with a reliable power grid. Poor infrastructure not only prevents local enterprises from being competitive but also deters foreign firms from locating facilities in the region.

Political considerations have driven African governments to spread infrastructure investments thinly. As a consequence of this, maintenance of facilities has been poor, both in places where established public services are underutilized and where there are shortages. In allocating resources for infrastructure development, governments face the dilemma of whether to focus on poverty alleviation or economic growth. The former requires spending in the poorest areas, while the latter calls for investment in the more dynamic parts of the country.

In market-oriented economies, the tendency is for all factors of production, including physical and human capital, to flow to the same places, making economic activity highly concentrated. For instance, most of the rapid economic growth that has taken place in China since the 1980s has occurred in a relatively small section of the country on the eastern coast. In the United States, counties that take up just 2 percent of the nation's land area account for half of its GDP.

UNEVEN DEVELOPMENT BETWEEN REGIONS

Divergence in prosperity between the few well-endowed areas of a country and the underdeveloped parts is a feature of modern economic development. Differences between levels of per capita income within Africa were minimal 200 years ago but have grown massively over the past century. With economic resources (especially physical and human capital) tending to bunch together in some locations, the rich benefit disproportionately. For example, by 1965 Lagos, with less than 4 percent of Nigeria's population, accounted for nearly 40 percent of the country's output in firms with more than 10 employees. It is not only wealth that is concentrated; so is poverty. In Africa, as elsewhere in the developing world, poverty is more acute in remote, sparsely populated rural areas, where the costs of providing modern services tend to be highest. Of course, large masses of poor exist in wealthy urban centers, but these people have more proximity and access to modern facilities such as electric power, transportation, and water than do the rural poor.

The concentration of wealth and poverty is not determined only by geographical factors; often it also has an ethnic dimension. In many African countries some ethnic groups tend to be more prosperous than others. For example, the Igbo in Nigeria, Kikuyu in Kenya, and Tutsi in Burundi and Rwanda are considered to be economically dominant ethnic groups in their respective countries.

Governments in Africa have endeavored to spread economic development more evenly across wide geographic and ethnic expanses. Poverty reduction programs aim to channel resources to the most underdeveloped areas of the country, especially for provision of essential services like education and health care. However, this has often meant allocating resources in ways that are not efficient from the point of view of achieving maximum output or utilization. For instance, building and operating electric power generators to serve a remote village is unlikely to be as

Africa emerged as a major focus of the 2005 annual meeting of the World Economic Forum in Davos, Switzerland. At this session—which included (from left) President Olusegun Obasanjo of Nigeria; Bill Clinton, former president of the United States; Bill Gates, chairman of Microsoft Corporation; and President Thabo Mbeki of South Africa—participants called for rich nations to cancel the debt of Africa's impoverished countries and to help fund health initiatives in the continent.

cost-effective as boosting power supply to urban and industrial centers.

However, the problem is not so much that African governments have set their investment priorities according to political and social considerations, but that for most of the time since independence they maintained state monopolies in economically crucial infrastructure sectors. As a result, there was little room for private investors to respond to the unmet demands for utilities such as power and communications in undersupplied areas. Government pricing policies were also set with little regard to commercial objectives, including cost recovery and proper maintenance of facilities.

Failure to take care of existing infrastructure is a major cause of the collapse or malfunctioning of services in most parts of Africa. The problem is not simply due to insufficient public funds, although this is a factor. In many countries governments are more inclined to budget money for new projects than to make provisions for the upkeep of existing facilities. In corruption-ridden states it is easier and more lucrative for officials to skim money from new and grand projects than to steal maintenance funds. Politicians are also more likely to win new supporters by being associated with the building of new roads or power plants than by ensuring that existing facilities run smoothly.

Furthermore, most African countries lack the local technical capabilities to properly maintain high-technology infrastructure, such as telecommunications and electric power networks. Often these facilities are installed by foreign companies, and once their initial service contracts run out, local owners struggle to keep them operating efficiently.

Although infrastructures throughout Africa are generally in poor condition by Western standards, significant variation exists among African countries. Countries with better government and more robust economies tend to have better-kept facilities. For instance, in South Africa the infrastructure available to the formal sector of the economy is generally of high quality. The post-apartheid government has also made strides in extending public services to South Africa's large informal sector—that is, businesses that are not registered with the government and avoid paying taxes. Between 1996 and 2000, the proportion of homes in the country with electric power rose from 55 percent to 70 percent. Significant progress in infrastructure provision has also been made in other well-governed states such as Botswana and Mauritius, where the percentage of roads in good condition is 94 percent and 95 percent respectively, according to the World Bank. By comparison, only 34 percent of the roads in Nigeria are in good condition, and the average for the whole continent is only slightly higher (39 percent).

SMALL FIRMS ARE NOT ALWAYS BEST

In developed countries, large companies and corporations employ the majority of non-farm workers. Most African countries have a few large companies, mainly foreign owned, and numerous very small firms operated by locals, with little in between. A dynamic small and medium-scale enterprises sector has developed in only a few countries, such as South Africa and Mauritius. Elsewhere, indigenous business is conducted by small enterprises operating mostly in the informal sector. Small enterprises provide not only the most substantial share of employment in all African countries, but also most of the everyday material needs of the poor. Many small enterprises prefer to remain in the informal sector, as this enables them to avoid the hassles of dealing with state agencies. But for most, their size reflects fundamental constraints that prevent them from growing.

One of the most cited obstacles to capital accumulation in Africa is the lack of access to finance. Micro and small companies have tended to be shut out of the formal sector financial system, often because they lack collateral. Limited access to finance not only hampers the growth of firms, but also prevents start-up of new ventures. Small entrepreneurs often lack the wherewithal to persuade banks to extend them credit. They lack collateral, and they are unable to comply with other prerequisites of financial institutions, such as the presentation of business plans and feasibility studies. Banks also tend to be wary of lending to small producers because of perceived high risks of doing so. Governments and non-bank financial institutions have established various schemes to lend money to small enterprises, but the amounts involved are usually too small to finance capital expansion.

Small enterprises have also failed to grow because of their low productivity. Small enterprises, whether in agriculture, services, or basic manufacturing, rely on basic tools, lack modern management, and are hampered by poor infrastructure. They usually cater to small markets and lack the means to expand their reach. Many are essentially subsistence or near-subsistence producers, concerned only with making enough to ensure the survival of their families.

Although small enterprises in the informal sector account for the bulk of employment in Africa, most are unable to pay living wages and often rely on

Ghanaian women stir thick paste by hand at the final stage of an extremely labor-intensive process for producing shea butter from the nuts of a tree indigenous to the savanna of West Africa. Since at least the 14th century, West African women have been making shea butter — which is today in great demand as an ingredient in cosmetics — using the same arduous process. Recently, however, some women have formed cooperatives, obtained loans, and purchased presses for crushing shea nuts. This has enabled them to increase production by more than 4,000 percent.

family members and apprentice labor. As such, they find it difficult to motivate workers to boost their output.

UNEMPLOYMENT AND UNDEREMPLOYMENT

Even when tiny enterprises are able to raise their productivity, in the majority of cases they still stand little chance of upgrading their operations to the levels needed to be competitive in the international market. Most modern production, including commercial farming, agribusiness, electronics, and information technology, requires firms with substantial amounts of capital—amounts that are well beyond the reach of the typical small African entrepreneur. Even labor-intensive activities, like making textiles, clothing, or shoes, need high levels of investment in physical and human capital to reach a globally competitive scale of operation.

Africa's small enterprises are simply not in a position to create the employment opportunities needed to uplift millions of unemployed and underemployed people from poverty. Unemployment and underemployment in Africa are largely structural in nature. They reflect the predominance of low-productivity, low-income, and subsistence-oriented firms, each with capacity to engage only a few workers. According to the Global Employment Trends 2003 report, produced by the International Labor Organization (ILO), almost 45 percent of the 271 million people employed in Africa in 2003 were "working poor," meaning they did not earn enough to provide decent living conditions for their families. The number of working poor is liable to increase in the region as its labor force increases from 271 million people in 2003 to an estimated 366 million in 2015. By then almost 50 percent of the total labor force will be living in urban areas. With a workforce growing by an estimated 2.5 percent a year, Africa needs to create nearly 8 million jobs annually until 2015 to absorb the rapidly growing number of job seekers.

According to the ILO, just to halve the number of unemployed and working poor by 2015 would require the rate of GDP growth to triple, which is a rather unrealistic goal for most African economies. To achieve these levels of economic expansion would require substantial investment in the establishment of modern firms. In a 1953 report on the prospects for industrialization in the Gold Coast—now Ghana—it was estimated that about 1,000 British pounds (£1,000) of capital investment would be required for each industrial worker's job created (this excluded many capital-intensive industries). Using this conservative estimate, a World Bank report on Nigeria in 1955 projected that the creation of enough new industries to engage an additional 1 percent of Nigeria's working population would demand an aggregate investment of £165 million, which was well beyond the scope of the indigenous private sector.

The report highlighted the obstacles to realizing such levels of investment with Nigerian private capital. First, investors are likely to show little interest in investment in industry as long as they are able to make quick profits in commercial transactions, which do not entail tying up funds over a long period and can be financed partly by bank credit. Second, few Africans are wealthy enough to finance, solely with their own resources, anything more than a small manufacturing enterprise. Third, the concept of the joint-stock company (by which a pool of individual investors purchase shares in an enterprise) is not familiar among Africans. Fourth, industrial credit is difficult to obtain. In the 1955 report, the World Bank observed that a shortage of private Nigerian venture capital was likely to constitute a severe limitation on financial participation in industrial development. Given the inadequacy of domestic capital to finance rapid industrial growth, the report said, Nigeria ought to make full use of foreign capital and the managerial and technological skills that accompany it.

Half a century after this report, the story remains roughly the same, except that the sizes of the indigenous labor forces have multiplied, while capital costs of creating modern jobs have also risen.

African businessmen remain largely unwilling or unable to invest in modern firms to engage in large-scale economic activities, especially manufacturing and services. A variety of reasons have been given for this, which mainly relate to Africa's appalling business environment. A combination of poor policies, deficient institutions, physical infrastructure problems, human resource issues, and harmful geographical features takes a toll on the efficiency with which different firms and industries operate. According to the World Bank's Doing Business Indicators, which compares business environments across countries, many African countries rank among the most difficult places in the world to do business. African countries that are reasonably encouraging to investment—such as Botswana, South Africa, and Zambia—are decidedly the exception; in the majority of nations on the continent, potential investors remain encumbered by unnecessary obstacles, including lengthy and costly administrative procedures. For instance, starting a business in Angola takes 146 days, and enforcing contracts requires 1,011 days. In the Democratic Republic of the Congo, the cost of starting a business is six times the average income per capita, and closing a business takes more than five years. The combination of macroeconomic instability, red tape, weak institutions, and poor infrastructure has pushed up indirect costs associated with productive activities to levels that undermine productivity and profits.

Although the business environment in Africa is awful and deters investment in new industries, the problem facing the region goes beyond red tape. Indeed, the impact of the business environment has sometimes been exaggerated. When China began its economic push in the late 1970s, its business environment was in many respects as bad as conditions found in Africa today. In 1996 China ranked only four places above Nigeria (which occupied the bottom place) in Transparency International's Corruption Perception Index. Even today, many African countries perform better than the Asian economic giant in several economic freedom indexes. For instance, in the Heritage Foundation's Index of Economic Freedom 2005, 13 sub-Saharan countries were deemed to be freer than China. While China is ranked as mostly un-free, African states such as Botswana, South Africa, Mauritius, and Senegal are mostly free.

TECHNOLOGY CAPABILITIES AND DEVELOPMENT

The problem facing African countries is not so much the lack of investment but the inability to effectively utilize available factors of production, especially physical and human capital. Africa's predicament is low productivity, rather than insufficient numbers of factories. Indeed, some economists contend that investment in Africa is too high rather than too low. A major indication of this is the low industrial capacity utilization in enterprises (state owned as well as private sector) throughout much of the continent.

According to the United Nations Economic Commission for Africa, manufacturing capacity utilization in Nigeria was 34.5 percent, and in Zimbabwe about 54 percent, in 2000. Both of these African nations, like most others on the continent, have seen the rate of usage of installed factory plants fall dramatically from the levels recorded in the 1960s and early 1970s. With existing modern industries operating well below full capacity, African businesspeople are not disposed to set up new firms to build even more factories. As a consequence, the industrial sector remains dominated by the subsidiaries of multinational companies, which are able to make profits despite their low levels of output, while indigenous businesspeople find few investment opportunities at home.

It is not entirely clear why productivity has declined in much of Africa during the past two decades after rising in the 1960s and early 1970s. A major factor, it seems, is the lack of an indigenous entrepreneurial class with the technological capability to operate modern firms in a competitive global market. Technological capability relates to the skill, dexterity, and judgment with which the factors of production, especially capital, are applied. For firms to succeed and grow, they must have this know-how; without the skills and information required to operate modern machinery and the learning ability to upgrade such skills when necessary, it is impossible to meet ever-changing consumer demand.

Technological capabilities can be categorized into three types: investment, production, and research and development (R&D).

The University of Kankan in Guinea celebrated the opening of its computer center in 2002. Because technology is expensive, many students do not have the opportunity to learn high-tech skills, and such skills are necessary in creating greater economic growth. The new center will allow the university to connect to the Internet and other learning institutions across the globe.

Investment capabilities relate to the firm's ability to identify and prepare feasible projects, procure suitable technologies, design and engineer the plant, and manage the construction. Production capabilities are the skills and knowledge needed for the subsequent operation, quality control, and improvement of the plant. R&D capabilities refers to the ability to learn and gain new knowledge that can augment the operation. Together, the three types of capabilities determine how effectively firms organize and manage their activities.

The dearth of African firms with high technological capabilities stems from a number of factors. First, government over-regulation of business activities has meant that entrepreneurs have been restricted in making investment and production decisions about location, form, and use of resources. For instance, regulations restricting the importation of certain production inputs undermine technological capabilities. This lack of economic freedom has stunted the growth of entrepreneurship in many parts of the region. Second, African countries are short of people with the skills needed for technologically driven development. Levels of scientific and engineering capabilities are quite low, as reflected in the low numbers of technology-related graduates in the continent. Third, most small African firms do not offer adequate on-the-job training for workers. Such training is an important contributor to higher value added by firms. According to the World Bank, an increase of just 1 percent in the number of workers trained could increase the value added by as much as 60 percent. Fourth, efforts at research and development within firms are both quantitatively and qualitatively minuscule. Fifth, political and social restrictions on the movement of people have prevented firms from acquiring technological capabilities they lack. Immigration controls, including expatriate quota limits, stop firms from employing technical consultants and experts from abroad. They also inhibit the migration to Africa of people with the entrepreneurial and technological abilities needed in the continent.

Perhaps the most important factor in the development of technological capabilities is the market. Firms develop technological capabilities through a process of trial and error and learning by doing. In a competitive environment, firms are compelled to become more efficient; otherwise they risk being knocked out of the market by better-managed rival producers.

Firms are driven by profits. They constantly strive to improve their systems of production to lower costs and reap the benefits of increasing returns. Higher sales create the potential for greater efficiency, the further lowering of production costs, increased leverage over suppliers, and heightened prospects for taking over a rival. In contrast, firms that are unable to improve their technological capabilities face increasing production costs and lower sales, creating a greater possibility that they will go bankrupt or be taken over by more successful rivals.

In an increasingly competitive global economy, Africa's low-productivity firms struggle to survive and lack the space to develop their technological capabilities. Larger and more efficient producers from other regions of the world, especially Asia, are not only outcompeting them in the international arena, but also dominating Africa's domestic markets.

This has been the case for many labor-intensive industries—the type Africa needs in order to create decent jobs for its large numbers of unemployed and working poor. Take, for instance, the clothing and textiles sectors, which are generally regarded as first-stage industries in the industrialization process. The prospects are slim that Africa will see a boost in domestic investment in these industries because highly efficient Asian companies dominate the markets.

Some African governments have tried to protect local industries against foreign competition by imposing import restrictions, but such policies have been undermined by smuggling. In Nigeria, for example, government bans on the importation of various types of textiles and clothing have not prevented the closure of dozens of factories, and the loss of tens of thousands of jobs. The culprit, according to Nigeria's textile and garment unions and manufacturers, is the widespread smuggling of textile materials from Asia, particularly China.

Africa has a number of mineral resources for which it has comparative advantage; it can produce them at a lower cost than competitors. For these commodities, such as oil, copper, and diamonds, African producers face little problem finding buyers for their output. But the exploitation of mineral wealth can support employment opportunities for only a small portion of Africa's labor force. For virtually all other types of economic activity,

Because they require large numbers of low-skill, low-wage workers, footwear and clothing manufacturing are typically viewed as first-stage industries for developing economies. Here, South African workers assemble shoes in a footwear factory.

including most agricultural production and services that do not require workers to be on location, African producers face international competition. Even in the production of African cultural artifacts, local producers have had to contend with manufacturers in Asia that mass-produce African objects for international markets.

Today there is global production overcapacity in most labor-intensive industries that African countries might develop. With firms in all regions striving to boost their output, production everywhere is running ahead of consumption. There is fierce competition between producers for the existing markets, involving not only developing countries but also the developed world. Whether it is cotton, clothing, shoes, steel, or DVD players, companies across all continents are struggling to maintain and increase their share of the market. In this highly competitive environment, individuals and firms with the technological capabilities to produce efficiently have the best chance to survive and prosper.

CREATIVE DESTRUCTION AND MODERNIZATION

A growing number of economists have identified technological capabilities as the major factor explaining differences in levels of productivity between and across regions in the world. The new thinking focuses on technology and human capital as engines of growth. Modern development is not about endowment in natural resources and raw labor, but about the application of new and improved tools, machines, materials, and processes to achieve material objectives. It is about productivity.

The rapid and sustained economic growth seen in East Asia during the past four decades reflects sustained increases in productivity stemming from growth in technological capabilities. Asian countries have shown an openness to innovation. They have learned new ways of doing things and in the process abandoned old and less effective methods. This is what the Austrian economist Joseph Schumpeter described as "creative destruction." The idea is that every innovation and new idea undermines and overthrows the existing cultural and technological order. However, out of this "destruction" of the status quo arises the "creative" force that transforms the social and economic structure into the new status quo, which will last until a new innovation sets the process into motion again. Schumpeter saw innovation by entrepreneurs as the force that drives economic growth. Numerous types of innovation generate creative destruction, including new ways to organize production, new management methods, new sources of raw material, and new methods of marketing.

If the economically vibrant countries of East Asia have embraced capitalism and integration into the global economy—and are continually undergoing the process of creative destruction—African societies have been largely resistant to change. Most African farmers cultivate roughly the same types of crops, using the same methods, for the same markets as their predecessors did during the colonial era. Even though the evidence indicates that growing more cocoa, coffee, or cotton or digging for more copper is unlikely to produce much reward, communities remain fixed to these traditional activities. Although Africans want the benefits of modernization, many remain resistant to abandoning their static way of life and embracing a dynamic approach to growth.

The process of economic change brought about through innovation did not occur in East Asia by accident. Rather, it was the result of the intervention of modernizing elites. Japan provides the earliest example. After centuries of self-imposed isolation, feudal Japan was forced in the mid-1800s to open itself to trade with the technologically superior West. This humiliating interaction ultimately led to the toppling of Japan's military government (the Tokugawa shogunate) and the reinstitution of the monarchy (the Meiji restoration). The ruling class showed great determination to close the gap with the industrialized West, changing the face of Japanese education and acquiring Western technology. In scarcely more than a generation, Japan emerged from feudalism and was on the road to becoming an industrial power. About a century later, in the early 1960s, General Park Chung-hee of South Korea launched a major initiative to industrialize and modernize his society, whose traditional ways had remained largely unchanged for centuries. In China beginning in the late 1970s, the ruling Communist Party, after unsuccessful attempts to modernize the country through central planning, launched into capitalist development with the mission of making the Asian giant a world leader in high-technology production. Throughout East Asia's industrializing nations, the prime strategy of the ruling elites was the acquisition of technological capabilities. To this end, East Asian governments promoted policies favoring entrepreneurial activities. The state may have retained tight political control in many of the countries, but it allowed greater economic freedom, enabling individuals and enterprises to make decisions on how best to use their resources in the pursuit of profit.

A major factor in the development of technological capabilities was the introduction of competition. Individuals and enterprises with the attributes to succeed in their line of endeavor were able to do so and benefited from the fruits of their labor or investment. The presence of competition imposes an obligation to strive. It also fosters selection by merit, which is vital for building the competence of any organization.

In the process of adapting these capabilities, societies that seemed entrenched in conservative traditional culture have been radically transformed. These changes have not occurred as a result of targeted policies of cultural change but mainly as a result of economic innovation. East Asia's modernizing elites were driven by both the desire for personal wealth and power and a sense of nationalism fueled by the aspiration to match the West in economic power.

Africa's ruling elites have not shown similar determination. They have tended to perceive economic development mainly as a process of capital accumulation. But merely building new factories with the latest machinery will not necessarily result in high productivity and economic growth. Growth requires management skills and practices that result in the efficient combination of resources at the level of the firm. It also requires workers with the appropriate skills and knowledge to operate their machinery as well as the learning ability to improve their skills. There is little point in acquiring new technologies in the absence of a workforce able to use those technologies properly.

CULTURE IS NOT THE PROBLEM

Some people believe that culture is a major determining factor in the capacity of different groups to develop. According to this view, Africa's failure to progress is a result of its culture not being conducive to economic growth. This proposition is mistaken for a number of reasons. First, the notion that there is an African culture is questionable. Africa is not a homogeneous entity but a region with a huge variety of religions, customs, languages, and living styles. Second, what is commonly defined as "African culture" reflects values that are associated with all traditional societies. The values and beliefs most commonly attributed to African culture include communalism, extended family, collective identity, acceptance of authority, superstition, animism, and fatalism. Most of these values and institutions, which are at variance with the individualism and materialism of capitalism, are traits found in different forms in Europe before the

Industrial Revolution. It was the rise of capitalism that brought social transformation in European societies. The values associated with Chinese culture—including strong family ties, condemnation of pure profit-seeking, group orientation, respect for authority, and spirituality—are similar to traditional values found in other regions of the world. Nevertheless, entrepreneurs and entrepreneurship have flourished in contemporary Chinese societies despite a collectivist traditional culture that, if not antithetical to individualistic capitalism, is not supportive of it.

Undoubtedly, some cultural features of African societies do obstruct economic growth. One of these is communalism—the strong devotion to the interests of one's own ethnic group rather than society as a whole. Communalism in Africa has not only led to numerous bloody conflicts but also encouraged corruption and hindered the efficient flow of resources within African countries. It has fostered the belief that an individual's wealth stems from entitlement as a member of a particular group, rather than from the individual's own effort. Studies have found that hard work, thrift, honesty, and openness to strangers play an important role in economic growth.

Nevertheless, though culture can offer some insight into national development, differences in the economic prosperity of nations cannot be attributed primarily to supposed differences in "national character." Nor is culture a changeless factor. Cultures evolve. Beliefs and practices that have long existed in a society can change over one or two generations. This is key to understanding the process of creative destruction. Innovation is by definition the introduction of new ideas, goods, and practices that can change the status quo and change human development.

In the early stages of China's transition to capitalism, entrepreneurs in the country faced obstacles with which their counterparts in Africa are all too familiar. They encountered political and legal uncertainties stemming from the volatility of government policy; insecure property rights and weak rule of law; opaque regulations; and unpredictable courts. Chinese entrepreneurs had little access to bank credit. Most financed their operations from personal or family savings. There was also a lack of skilled labor. Many of these problems persist today, despite the economic strides made by the country.

Some African cultural nationalists suggest that capitalism cannot flourish on the continent because Africa's culture is intrinsically non-materialistic. This view is not substantiated by history. For many centuries trading networks linked African communities stretching from the southern part of the continent to the north (and even beyond). The trans-Saharan trade between Mediterranean countries and West Africa was an important trade route between the 8th century and the 16th century. Although the trans-Atlantic slave trade was a morally despicable affair, it nevertheless demonstrated the entrepreneurship of the Africans who were actively involved in the business. Many Africans became rich through the trade, especially in Nigeria and along the Slave Coast. They were clearly driven by the desire for material gain.

BRIGHT SPOTS ON THE INDUSTRIAL FRONT

Although industrialization appears to have passed most of Africa by, certain industries have operated profitably in many parts of the continent. These industries—including food processing, beverage bottling, and beer brewing—tend to involve products with large domestic demand and high transportation costs for imported substitutes.

One of Africa's best-performing industries is beer brewing. South African Breweries has grown to become one of the world's largest non-financial transnational corporations based in a developing country. The company operates in several African countries as well as in the United States, Central America, Asia, and Europe. East African Breweries has also done well, seeing its profits rise by 142 percent in the 2003–2004 financial year. In Nigeria, Guinness and Nigeria Breweries have prospered despite the country's difficult business environment.

Although the prospect of industrialization looks bleak in most parts of Africa, some areas have the potential for industrial transformation. South Africa's economy, the continent's largest, has been relatively well managed, with low inflation, little indebtedness, and a strong currency. It is a diversified economy, with manufacturing accounting for some 20 percent of GDP and agriculture only 4 percent.

Because of its official policy of apartheid, which mandated racial separation and discriminated against its nonwhite majority, South Africa was largely isolated by the international community. Economic sanctions were imposed, and many Western firms and investors withdrew their assets from South Africa. In some respects, South Africa actually benefited from this isolation, which compelled local companies to look inward. With the opening up of the economy since the end of apartheid in 1994, the country's economic prospects have improved. South Africa is the main source of outward foreign direct investment in the continent and has been making inroads to other African countries, furthering regional integration.

Nevertheless, South Africa still faces formidable challenges, such as how to rapidly reduce chronic poverty among the black majority without destabilizing the formal economic sector, which continues to be dominated by whites. In addition, the business climate—though less unfavorable than elsewhere in Africa—suffers from lengthy administrative processes and over-regulation. Shortage of skilled labor and the AIDS pandemic are also major obstacles to economic growth at levels sufficient to absorb unemployment and eradicate poverty.

6 GLOBALIZATION: A LEVEL PLAYING FIELD?

The increased integration of the world's economies during recent years has generated much debate and controversy in all regions of the globe. Supporters of globalization contend that the removal of barriers to the cross-country flow of goods, services, and labor has, by and large, been a positive development, bringing increased wealth and prosperity to all nations, even if some have gained more than others. Opponents argue that globalization has made poor nations poorer by reinforcing their underdevelopment and dependence on low-yielding primary products.

Observers on either side of the divide cite different statistics to support their cases. Pro-globalists, for instance, point out that the proportion of the world's people living below the poverty line of one dollar a day has shrunk. Opponents counter with figures that show a growing divergence in national incomes: in 1820 per capita income was about 3 times higher in the world's richest nation, Great Britain,

than in the world's poorest, China; by 1992 the gap between richest (the United States) and poorest (Ethiopia) stood at 72 to 1.

AFRICA BEHIND IN RACE FOR MARKETS

Both sides have a case. While it is not entirely accurate to say that under globalization the rich have gotten richer and the poor have gotten poorer, it is true that the rich have gotten richer at a much faster rate than the poor have gotten less poor. During the period 1960–1992, for instance, income growth in the poorest one-fifth of countries averaged 1.4 percent annually, compared with a rate of 2.2 percent in the richest one-fifth of countries. But the real question that faces impoverished Africans is whether trade has increased their poverty and whether they would be better off opting out of the global capitalist market, as suggested by some anti-globalization observers.

The experiences of materially prosperous nations strongly suggest that trade is necessary for rapid economic growth. No nation has developed in isolation. Africa's problem is not that its nations have traded too much, but that they have not traded enough—a situation reflected by the drop in the continent's share of world trade, from 3.7 percent in 1913, during the colonial period, to around 2 percent today.

The links between Africa's poverty and low trade are clear. Besides food and basic shelter, virtually all other goods and amenities wanting in Africa's poor communities require the importation of capital goods, such as machinery, that the continent currently lacks the capacity to produce. For example, it is inconceivable for underdeveloped countries to expand the provision of electricity, modern communications, or modern medicine without importation from more advanced nations.

Additionally, markets in Africa are too small to support large-scale production of most goods, making exports essential not only as a means of paying for imports but also as a means to promote industrial production.

In spite of whatever misgivings African leaders express about the global economic order, virtually all their countries aspire to increase their international trade, especially exports. But it has proved difficult for them to move beyond selling primary products for which they have comparative advantage. This has led to complaints that the global trading system is tilted against poor nations.

Developing-nation governments complain that subsidies paid by rich-nation governments to their farmers—totaling about $1 billion a day—result in overproduction and export dumping (exportation of crops or other products at a price below the cost of production). Subsidies thus suppress world prices and put at a disadvantage producers whose governments do not pay them subsidies. For example, subsidies paid by the U.S. government to cotton growers have been hurting Africa's cotton producers. Cotton is one of the main sources of livelihood in many West African countries. It accounts for 5 to 9 percent of GDP in Mali, Chad, Benin, Burkina Faso, and Togo, and cotton production provides employment to as much as one-third of the population. World cotton prices declined by about 30 percent in 2004, mainly because of increased output from China and the United States, and at the reduced prices African growers could not make a profit. Similarly, world sugar prices are kept artificially low by the heavy subsidies that European states pay to their producers, and this distortion of the market causes disadvantages to growers in poor nations.

Many developed nations acknowledge that their farm subsidies can have trade-distorting impacts harmful to poor Third World farmers, but have nevertheless been slow to reform their agricultural policies. The indications are that competition in international commodities trade will continue to be keen in the coming years. In its Agricultural Outlook report published in June 2005, the Organization for Economic Co-operation and Development (OECD) and the United Nations Food and Agriculture Organization said global competition among exporters of wheat, rice, oilseeds, sugar, and livestock is expected to intensify between 2005 and 2014. Stiff competition, combined with higher productivity, is expected to result in a further drop in real prices for most commodities.

ACCESS TO RICH-NATION MARKETS

Developing nations also complain that some of their exports face market barriers in rich countries, hampering their efforts to diversify their economies and reduce poverty. These barriers include high import tariffs on the types of processed and manufactured goods developing countries produce, like textiles and clothing, as well as non-tariff obstacles such as quality standards and technical barriers to trade. This sort of protectionism has hindered a few African countries, but for the most part the countries affected have been middle-income nations and large developing countries with big export sectors, such as China. For most poor African nations, market access is not a major problem, as their exports have benefited from trade preferences offered by industrialized countries to poor nations since the 1970s.

Under more recent initiatives, like the U.S. African Growth and Opportunity Act (AGOA) and the European Union's Everything But Arms (EBA) schemes, African producers have tariff-free access to Western markets for a wide range of goods. The AGOA, enacted in May 2000, gives sub-Saharan African countries increased preferential access to the U.S. market on condition that they improve macroeconomic policies and implement structural reforms. By 2005 three-quarters of the region's 48 countries had qualified for the preferences. The EBA abolished

U.S. secretary of state Condoleezza Rice and President Abdoulaye Wade of Senegal meet at the 2005 African Growth and Opportunity Act Forum in Dakar, Senegal. Thirty-seven African countries are eligible for duty-free trade rights with the United States under the act.

tariffs and quotas on imports of all goods, except arms, that originate from least developed countries, which includes most of sub-Saharan Africa.

Some African countries have managed to boost their manufacturing exports, especially textiles and clothing. Textiles and clothing represent a significant share of the total merchandise exports of nine African countries: Burkina Faso, Cape Verde, Lesotho, Madagascar, Malawi, Mauritius, Niger, Swaziland, and Zimbabwe.

However, despite the AGOA and EBA initiatives, sub-Saharan Africa's share of total world exports of textiles and clothing remains negligible, at less than 1 percent. One reason for this is that other countries in every developing region have also built textile and clothing industries as the first stage of accelerated industrialization. Textile and clothing production requires a large supply of low-skilled labor but often employs only simple technology, so it is a sector in which developing countries have a comparative advantage and can generate many jobs. Since the 1960s, developing countries' share of textile and clothing exports has risen substantially, yet the share in these exports by developing nations in sub-Saharan Africa stands at less than 2 percent.

Textile and garment exports from Africa expanded mainly on the basis of special preferences, especially the quota system established in 1974 by the Multi-Fibre Arrangement (MFA). The MFA limited the amount of textile and garment goods that China could ship into Western markets. This led Chinese investors from the mainland, Hong Kong, and Taiwan to set up plants in other regions with low-cost labor, including Africa. However, with the lapse of the MFA in January 2005 and China's accession to the World Trade Organization, there is concern that the East Asian transnational corporations responsible for much of the increases in sub-Saharan Africa's textile and apparel production may wind down their African activities and relocate back home.

Though sub-Saharan Africa has some of the lowest wages in the world, it has not attracted investment for other labor-intensive industries, such as footwear, toys, sporting goods, and electronics; investment in those industries has gone into other developing regions. Africa's inability to benefit from globalization stems largely from its current low levels of productivity. Low absolute wages do not count for much if the output of workers cannot stand up to foreign competition in terms of both quantity and quality. Production costs have remained higher in Africa than elsewhere in the world, although productivity has improved a little since the mid-1990s.

The evidence strongly suggests that the fundamental obstacle to economic growth in Africa is inadequate technological capability in activities that face foreign competition. Since improved transportation and communications have flattened the world more than ever before, global competition affects virtually all goods and most services. Even resource-based manufacturing does not guarantee a competitive edge for countries endowed with raw materials. For example, the fact that Nigeria produces crude oil does not mean that its poorly managed refineries can produce petroleum products at a cost lower than the cost of imported fuel.

Nevertheless, African countries that have opened up their economies and focused on trade above other endeavors have tended to do better than those that have remained inward looking. Mauritius, for example, has succeeded in moving from a sugar-based economy into a well-diversified, fast-growth economy with manufacturing exports and a tourism sector, in the process transforming itself from a very poor country into one whose citizens enjoy a per capita income that is well above the average for developing nations. The island's success has been due to a number of factors, including good governance, stable and democratic regimes, and sensible economic policies, such as

Lovely beaches like this one help draw more than half a million visitors to Mauritius each year. But the island nation's vibrant economy is based on more than tourism. A well-established agricultural sector and growing industrial and financial sectors give Mauritius a diversified economy. The country's 1.2 million citizens enjoy one of Africa's highest per capita incomes—testimony to the economic benefits that can come from stability, good governance, a democratic tradition, and farsighted development policies.

establishment of export processing zones (EPZs) and encouragement of foreign investment. EPZs are areas where companies producing for export markets enjoy certain concessions and pay no import duties. In 2003 EPZ manufacturing accounted for 10 percent of the GDP and almost 60 percent of the total exports of Mauritius, while employing 17 percent of the country's workforce. In 2005 the government announced plans to turn the whole island into a duty-free zone to further boost its export trade.

Other countries that have successfully used EPZs include Lesotho and Madagascar. The former is a rare case of a landlocked country whose economy has done reasonably well in the export markets. Some 70 percent of its exports are manufactured goods, well above the average of 25 percent for Africa as a whole.

7 THE SEARCH FOR SOLUTIONS

For more than 30 years, politicians, analysts, and development activists inside and outside of Africa have searched for solutions to the region's economic woes. Not surprisingly, the remedies offered have varied with differing assessments of the nature of the ailment. Nationalist-oriented Africans and anticapitalist thinkers who blame Africa's plight primarily on external factors—such as the legacy of colonialism, unfair international trading, and high foreign debt—tend to see the region's redemption in withdrawal from global capitalism. This would require that African countries not only reinforce existing barriers to international trade with advanced countries, but also erect new ones. However, most African leaders regard models of self-sufficient development as unrealistic and impractical.

THE CASE FOR MORE AID

By contrast, anti-poverty campaigners who believe that Africa's problems stem mainly from

(Opposite) Nigerian president Olusegun Obasanjo addresses the New Partnership for Africa's Development 2005 summit in Sharm el-Sheikh, Egypt. In August of that year, the organization received an award for its progress in bringing satellite broadband Internet connections to schools across Africa.

lack of money to invest in poverty reduction have urged rich nations to increase development aid and debt relief to the region to fill its resource gap. The New Partnership for Africa's Development, launched in 2002, says Africa needs to fill an annual resource gap of $64 billion to rebuild the continent. The 2005 report from the Commission for Africa, which was set up by Prime Minister Tony Blair of the United Kingdom, recommended that aid to Africa be doubled to $50 billion a year over the next 10 years.

After having fallen from $17 billion in 1990 to $10 billion in 2001, official development aid to sub-Saharan Africa increased. In 2003 total development aid stood at $24.1 billion, or $34 per person on the continent. Africa is the world's most aid dependent region; foreign support accounts for more than a quarter of the national incomes of at least seven nations.

Advocates of increased aid also want the rich nations to forgive sub-Saharan Africa's external debt, which totaled $231 billion in 2003. African governments and international aid agencies say that servicing this debt, much of which was incurred under corrupt former regimes, is an enormous drain on the region's meager resources. Even after implementing various debt reduction schemes introduced by creditor institutions during the past two decades, Africa still pays out more in debt service than it spends on education.

Debt-forgiveness advocates won a partial victory in 2005, when the Group of Eight (G8)—the leading industrial nations plus Russia—put forth a proposal to cancel the external debts of 18 countries, 14 of them in Africa. The World Bank and the International Monetary Fund (IMF) later agreed to this proposal.

The World Bank and the IMF have been generally sympathetic to the demands of African states and anti-poverty non-governmental organizations (NGOs) for increased financial flows to poor African nations. However, the two international finance institutions make development assistance to indebted poor countries conditional on their governments' implementation of economic liberalization reforms. These reforms aim to improve government macroeconomic policies and restructure

Paul Wolfowitz, president of the World Bank, participates in a roundtable discussion on strategies for reducing poverty in Africa. At left is Faida Mitifu, the Democratic Republic of the Congo's ambassador to the United States; at right is Rosa Whitaker, a consultant specializing in African Growth and Opportunity Act law.

the economy to lessen state control and promote free enterprise. They were initially introduced in the mid-1980s in the form of the Structural Adjustment Program (SAP). Most African states signed up for the program, which included devaluation of over-valued national currencies, financial liberalization, tax reforms, privatization of inefficient state enterprises, removal of barriers to foreign investment, and trade liberalization.

Development economists differ in their assessments of the impact of SAP on troubled economies in Africa and elsewhere in the developing world. While some claim that it spurred economic growth in countries that implemented the reforms properly, others contend that it made little difference anywhere. In 1999 the World Bank and IMF replaced SAP with the Poverty Reduction Strategy Paper (PRSP), which retains macroeconomic and structural reforms but also gives some weight to social policies and emphasizes the national ownership of adopted strategies.

SHORTAGE OF MONEY IS NOT THE MAIN PROBLEM

A major drawback of many approaches to Africa's development predicament is the assumption that the crisis is due to a lack of capital. While international aid groups demand that rich nations pump more money into the region, Western governments and international finance institutions want African governments to better manage the resources available to them. Both perspectives have merit in that Africa will need more capital and much improved state economic management to radically reduce poverty, but at the moment the region's problem does not stem from lack of capital.

African nations are clearly poor and have low levels of savings, but much of the savings that exist in the region are not being invested in wealth creation locally. Around 40 percent of

African savings are kept outside the continent, compared with just 6 percent for East Asia and 3 percent for South Asia. According to the United Nations Economic Commission for Africa, capital flight from 30 African countries over the period 1970–1996 amounted to $187 billion. For eight sub-Saharan African countries, including Angola and Nigeria, the ratio of capital-flight stock to GDP exceeds 2 to 1. In other words, the accumulated value of private assets shifted abroad is twice the value of all goods and services produced domestically per year.

The loss of capital is partly due to corruption, but it also reflects lack of confidence and want of investment opportunities. Capital flight may be seen as a portfolio choice made by people who believe that keeping their assets at home is too risky or yields insufficient returns. With wealthy Africans not investing their assets at home, it is unsurprising that foreign investment in Africa is low. In the 1960s Africa received the highest share of foreign direct investment (FDI) of all developing regions but has since fallen behind. The region's share of FDI has declined over time, from about 19 percent in the 1970s to 7 percent in the 1980s and about 3 percent in the 1990s. In 2003 sub-Saharan Africa received FDI totaling only about $10 billion, much of it going to extractive industries—mostly oil and gas—in a few countries, including Angola, Equatorial Guinea, and Nigeria.

Although foreign investment in Africa is low, private domestic investment in the region is also much less than it could be, judging from the high levels of capital flight from some African countries. This suggests that African governments need to pursue policies that will encourage private investment from both domestic and foreign sources. This will involve removing restrictions that hamper producers from managing their resources in an efficient manner.

 # CONCLUSION

n seeking to implement reforms that might foster environments more conducive to wealth creation by their own people, African leaders face a daunting task. The 21st century holds mixed opportunities for the inhabitants of poor nations striving to escape poverty by developing their production capabilities. On the one hand, vast improvements in technology (and greater access to it) since the mid-20th century make it easier for individuals and firms in the underdeveloped parts of the world to catch up with the levels of capability in advanced nations. On the other hand, the new century has shown signs of being marked by intensive economic competition between the peoples and nations of the world—poor and rich. With some 3 billion people on the globe struggling to escape poverty and the citizens of rich countries facing the economic challenges of emergent nations, particularly China and India, global competition for markets and jobs is bound to become much stiffer.

NO PANACEA

Despite signs of increased willingness on the part of African rulers, rich-nation governments, and international development institutions to address the issue of African poverty, nobody has come up with a panacea for treating the problem. This is probably because none exists. For instance, increasing aid and market access for poor countries makes sense, but the extent to which this leads to poverty reduction will depend on how beneficiary countries use the extra funds and whether they have the production capacity to exploit new market opportunities. Some people and societies will be better at responding to market signals than others.

Economic history teaches us that development is something largely determined by poor countries themselves. Outsiders can play only a limited role. Similarly, within poor nations development is not something that governments can do for the poor. Government has a vital but limited role to play—basically that of fostering an environment in which people can engage in productive activities, securely and without unnecessary interference or hindrance. Under the right conditions, principally freedom and security, workers and entrepreneurs will take the steps necessary to achieve wealth and prosperity for themselves and their families.

The main challenge facing African governments is to improve their countries' business

Despite efforts by governments, international organizations, charities, and humanitarian groups, the problem of poverty in Africa persists.

environments so that modern competitive enterprises can emerge and grow, generating decent-wage job opportunities. Competition between individuals and firms vying for markets at home and abroad is a necessary condition for improving indigenous technological capabilities. Companies innovate in response to competitive pressure.

Development is ultimately something the poor do for themselves, and this process is best achieved through trade relations within the global economy. There is truth in the cliché that the poor must trade themselves out of poverty. Calls for national economics, as opposed to globalized economics, are misguided for a number of reasons. First, producers in Africa need much larger markets to grow and specialize. The tiny size of most internal markets is a major obstacle to economic development and poverty reduction in most African nations. Second, no developing country will have access to the world's advanced technologies without trade. Most, if not all, the deprivations that characterize African poverty require imported technology to solve, including electricity, modern health care, and motorized transportation. Third, as consumers, the poor are able to get more for their little incomes when they have access to the global market.

The claim by critics of globalization that integration in the international economy is responsible for Africa's endemic poverty is patently wrong. Though the region's share of world trade has shrunk during the past three decades, Africans have nevertheless benefited from globalization. An obvious illustration is that poor Africans, even in some of the most remote villages, now have access to a wide range of low-cost manufactured goods from China, such as clothing and kitchen utensils, which without foreign trade would have remained well beyond their reach. When measured in terms of income growth, many African nations appear to have made little or no progress in the past few decades, but this is not the case when conditions are viewed according to social indicators such as school enrollment, immunization, and access to clean water and electricity.

Africa has benefited from globalization, but not as much as other regions or by as much as it could have. It is true that for millions of Africans handicapped for life by lack of health care, educational opportunities, and decent jobs, globalization has made little difference. The challenge facing African governments, private sector organizations, and NGOs is to change this tragic reality by striving to boost Africa's place in the global economy.

GLOSSARY

CAPACITY—the ability of individuals, organizations, and societies to perform functions, solve problems, and set and attain their objectives.

CAPITAL—assets used in the production of further assets, such as factories, equipment, and money.

COLONIALISM—the extension of a nation's sovereignty over territory and people outside its own boundaries.

COMPARATIVE ADVANTAGE—a position of relative superiority (for example, because of greater efficiency) that one producer (a country, firm, or individual) enjoys over another producer.

CORRUPTION—the misuse of power or public trust for private gain.

ECONOMIC GROWTH—the annual increase in a nation's total output of goods and services or the annual increase in the nation's total income.

ELITE—the privileged or ruling class of society.

FACTORS OF PRODUCTION—the ingredients of economic activity (land, labor, and capital).

FOREIGN DIRECT INVESTMENT—investment made by a foreign individual or company in productive capacity of another country (for example, the acquisition or construction of a factory).

FOREIGN EXCHANGE—the buying and selling of currencies used to make payments between countries.

GLOBAL PRODUCTION CHAIN—the linkage between the different firms engaged in the various stages in the production of a product.

GOVERNANCE—the processes and systems by which an organization or society is governed.

GROSS DOMESTIC PRODUCT (GDP)—the total value of goods and services produced in a country in a one-year period.

IMPERIALISM—the extension of rule or influence by one government, nation, or society over another.

INFLATION—persistent upward movement in the general price level.

INFORMAL ECONOMY—the part of the economy whose activities are unrecorded in national accounts and operated without regard to government rules.

INVESTMENT—property or other assets acquired in the hope of getting a future return or benefit from it.

INVESTMENT CLIMATE—the sum of local factors that shape the opportunities and incentives for firms to invest productively, create jobs, and expand.

LIBERALIZATION—relaxation of government restrictions, especially in the areas of social and economic policies.

MARKET—any place where sellers of particular goods and services meet buyers to carry out transactions.

PRODUCTIVITY—the rate at which goods and services are produced, especially per unit of labor.

PURCHASING POWER PARITY (PPP)—an exchange rate that accounts for price differences across countries, allowing for international comparison of real output and income.

REAL CAPITAL—capital, such as equipment and machinery, used to produce goods, as distinguished from financial capital (funds to acquire real capital).

STATISM—the doctrine or system in which government implements a significant degree of central economic planning.

TRANSNATIONAL CORPORATION—a business enterprise with manufacturing, sales, or service subsidiaries in one or more foreign countries.

VALUE—an amount of goods, services, or money that is considered to be a fair equivalent for something else.

GLOSSARY

FURTHER READING

Akyuz, Yilmaaz, and Charles Gore. *African Development in a Comparative Perspective*. Oxford: James Currey Publishers, 2000.

Brown, Michael Barratt. *Africa's Choices: After Thirty Years of the World Bank*. Middlesex, UK: Penguin Books, 1995.

Chabal, Patrick, and Jean-Pascal Daloz. *Africa Works: Disorder as Political Instrument*. Bloomington: Indiana University Press, 1999.

Commission for Africa. *Our Common Interest: Report of the Commission for Africa*. March 2005. http://www.commissionforafrica.org/english/report/introduction.html.

Guest, Robert. *The Shackled Continent*. London: MacMillan, 2004.

Timberlake, Lloyd. *Africa in Crisis: The Causes, the Cures of Environmental Bankruptcy*. 2nd edition. London: Earthscan, 1988.

World Bank, *Can Africa Claim the 21st Century?* Washington, D.C.: The World Bank, 2000. http://siteresources.worldbank.org/INTAFRICA/Resources/complete.pdf.

INTERNET RESOURCES

HTTP://WWW.UNECA.ORG

The website of the Economic Commission for Africa, the regional arm of the UN in Africa, contains useful studies on different aspects of economic and social development in the continent.

HTTP://WWW.NEPAD.ORG

The website of the New Partnership for Africa's Development, a blueprint agreed to by African leaders for Africa's renewal, has material reflecting the perspective of African governments on development and poverty.

HTTP://WWW.WORLDBANK.ORG/AFR/

The Africa section of the World Bank site is rich with statistics and analysis on a variety of topics related to development in sub-Saharan Africa.

HTTP://WWW.AFRICAECONOMICANALYSIS.ORG

Includes articles on economic and social issues in Africa.

HTTP://WWW.AFROBAROMETER.ORG

This site offers reports, based on the results of national sample surveys, on the attitudes of people in selected African countries toward different aspects of development.

HTTP://WWW.CSAE.OX.AC.UK

The website of the Center for the Study of African Economies, based at Oxford University, contains reports written by economists and social scientists.

INTERNET RESOURCES

HTTP://WWW.NATIONMASTER.COM

Allows users to select data to generate online maps and graphs for countries all over the world. Graphs can overlay economic data with other social, health, crime, or government issues to help identify correlations.

HTTP://WWW.WEFORUM.ORG

The World Economic Forum's website provides summaries of discussions based on region. The Global Competitiveness Report is also available by country.

Publisher's Note: The websites listed on this page were active at the time of publication. The publisher is not responsible for websites that have changed their address or discontinued operation since the date of publication. The publisher will review and update the websites each time the book is reprinted.

INDEX

absolute poverty, 15
   See also poverty
African Growth and
   Opportunity Act (AGOA),
   110–111
African Union, **106**
agriculture, 24–25, 59, 65–72,
   100
      genetically modified
         (GM) crops, 72–74
      subsidies, 20–21, 70,
         108–109
      See also environmental
         degradation
agrobiotechnology, 72–74
   See also agriculture
AIDS. *See* HIV/AIDS
Angola, 75, 93, 118
apartheid, 105

Bauer, Peter, 31
beer brewing, 104–105
   See also industrial
     development
Blair, Tony, 115
Botswana, 21, 56, 76, 82, 89,
   93, 94
brain drain, 59–61

See also capital

Cameroon, 47, 85
capital, 42–43, 46–47,
   117–118
      and exchange rates,
         43–46
      flight, 50, 117–118
      human, 19, 51–55, 57–61
      See also investment
capitalism
   and colonialism, 35–36
   and culture, 103–104
   See also market economy
Chad, 63
China, 79–80, 83, 86, 93–94,
   98, 101, 103–104, 111, 119
civil conflicts, 15, 38–40, **53**
   and natural resources,
     74–76
Clinton, Bill, **87**
colonialism, 15, 30–33, 37
   and capitalism, 35–36
   and economic development,
     67
   and industrial development,
     33–35
Commission for Africa, 115

Numbers in **bold italic** refer to captions.

INDEX

communalism, 103
   See also culture
communications, 83, 88
   See also infrastructure
corruption, 20, 41, 47–48, 74
   See also government
"creative destruction,"
   99–102, 103
    See also globalization
crime, 48, **49**
culture, 102–104
currency. *See* exchange rates

debt relief, 16, 115–117
   See also foreign aid
Democratic Republic of the
   Congo, 75, 85, 93
diamonds, **75**, 76, 82, 98
   See also natural resources
diversification, economic, 65,
   81–82, 105, 112
"Dutch disease," 75–76
   See also natural resources

East African Breweries, 105
education, 32, 51–55, 61
Elbadawi, Ibrahim, 39
entrepreneurial development,
   35–36, 90, 96
environmental degradation,
   20–21, 23–25
Equatorial Guinea, 63, **95**,
   118
Ethiopia, **33**, 37, 54, **68**
ethnic groups, 39, 86–87, 103

Everything But Arms (EBA),
   110–111
exchange rates, 43–46
   See also capital
export processing zones
   (EPZs), 112–113
exports, 79
   agricultural, 66–67
   and globalization, 81–83,
    107–113
   See also trade

Fieldhouse, D. K., 31
financing, 89–90, 92–94
   See also investment
firms, 36, 97
   small, 89–91
   See also capitalism
Food and Agriculture
   Organization, 25, 66, 109
foreign aid, 16, **55**, 61,
   114–117
foreign investment, 34,
   49–50, 92–94, 112, 118
   See also investment

Gates, Bill, **87**
genetically modified (GM)
   crops, 72–74
   See also agriculture
geography, 23–25
   See also environmental
    degradation
Ghana, 54, 92
Global Corruption Barometer

2004, 47
See also corruption
globalization, 97–100, 114,
119–122
  and "creative destruc-
    tion," 99–102, 103
  definition of, 17
  and exports, 81–83,
    107–113
  uneven benefits from,
    18–20, 106–109
  See also trade
gold, 75
See also natural resources
Gono, Gideon, ***46***
government
  corruption, 19–21, 41,
    47–50, 74
  and economic reform,
    120–122
  education funding, 54–55
  and exchange rates, 43–46
  investment of, in agricul-
    ture, 67–71
  investment of, in infra-
    structure, 84–86, 88–89
  and political instability,
    37–40, 48
  regulations, 20, 47, 93, 96
  and state-run enterprises,
    40–43
Great Britain, 26–27, 29
gross domestic product (GDP)
  African, 14, 21, 26–27, 37,
    65, 76–77

health care, 14, 55–59
Heritage Foundation, 94
HIV/AIDS, 14, 56–59, 105
*How Europe Underdeveloped
  Africa* (Rodney), 30
human capital, 19, 51–55,
  57–61
See also capital

incentive structure, 69–70
See also agriculture
independence, 13, 32–33,
  37–41
India, 68, 119
industrial development,
  33–35, 76–81, 94–95,
    104–105, 112–113
industrial revolution, 26–27
infrastructure, ***21***, 32, ***33***, 40,
  63, 83–86, 88–89
  and labor productivity,
    80
  See also technology
International Labor
  Organization (ILO), 91–92
investment, 48–49, 50, 88
  agricultural, 67–71
  foreign, 34, 49–50, 92–94,
    112, 118
  infrastructure, 84–86,
    88–89
  See also capital
Ivory Coast, 85

Japan, 100–101

Johnson, Samuel, 29–30

Kenya, 47, 54, 59, 60

labor migration, 60–61
    See also capital
labor productivity, 79–80,
    94–95, 99
        See also industrial
            development
Lagos, 86
Lake Chad, **69**
land reform, 71–72
    See also agriculture
Lesotho, **38**, 56, 79, 113
Liberia, 37
life expectancy, 14, 56
literacy rates, 52
    See also education

Madagascar, 113
Maddison, Angus, 62
malaria, 58–59
Mali, 63
manufacturing, 76–81, 94–95,
    104–105, 112–113
market economy, 19, 36, 86
    and exchange rates, 43–46
Mauritius, 21, 77, 79, 89, 94,
    112–113
Mbeki, Thabo, **87**
Millennium Development
    Goals, 14, 53–54, 59
Mitifu, Faida, **116**
Mkhize, Mthembeni, **18**

Mozambique, 32
Multi-Fibre Arrangement
    (MFA), 111

natural resources, 48, **49**,
    74–76, 98–99
New Partnership for Africa's
    Development, **114**, 115
Niger, 52, 63
Nigeria, 29–30, **31**, **49**, 54,
    75, 85, 92, 98, 118
        agriculture in, 66, 68
        corruption in, 47–48
        HIV/AIDS infection rate,
            56
        industrial development
            in, 33–34, 94, 105
        infrastructure in, 89
        per capita income in,
            78–79

Obasanjo, Olusegun, **87**, **114**
oil, 48, **49**, 74, 76, 98
    See also natural resources
Organization for Economic
    Co-operation and
        Development (OECD),
            109
Organization of African
    Unity, 38

population, 14, 78–79
    growth, 61–64, 81
Portuguese colonialism, 32
    See also colonialism

poverty
causes of, in Africa, 15–16,
20–22, 30–34
concentration of, 86–88
definition of, 15
and geography, 23–25
number of Africans living
in, 14
reduction programs, 87–88,
116–117, 119–121
Poverty Reduction Strategy
Paper (PRSP), 117
primary products, 65, 82–83
See also diversification,
economic
property rights, 70–72
See also agriculture

regulations, 20, 47, 93, 96
See also government
relative poverty, 15
See also poverty
remittances, 61
Republic of Korea, 13–14, 54
Rice, Condoleezza, **110**
Rodney, Walter, 30
Rwanda, **80**

Sambanis, Nicolas, 39
Sao Tome and Principe, 63
Schumpeter, Joseph, 35–36,
100
"Scramble for Africa," 30
See also colonialism
Senegal, 94

shea butter, **90**
Sierra Leone, 22, **53**, **75**, 76
slave trade, 15, 27–30, 104
small firms, 89–91
See also firms
small markets, 77–81, 108,
121
socialism, 40
See also government
Soto, Hernando de, 71
South Africa, 21, **41**, 52, 54,
56, 72, 73, 77, **78**, 79, 82,
85, 89, 93, 94, 105
South African Breweries,
104–105
statism, 40–43
See also government
Structural Adjustment
Program (SAP), 116–117
See also debt relief
subsidies, agricultural, 20–21,
70, 108–109
See also agriculture
Swaziland, 56

Tanzania, 54, 85
technology, 21, 88–89, 119
and "creative destruction,"
99–102, 103
development of, in Africa,
15, 94–99, 112
and globalization, 17–19
See also infrastructure
tourism, 112, **113**
trade

Africa's share of world, 66, 107–109, 112–113
barriers to, 81, 98, 109–111, 114
See also globalization
Transparency International, 47, 94
tuberculosis, 58–59

Uganda, 83–84
underemployment, 91–92, 97
unemployment, 91–92, 97
United Nations
    Development Program
        Human Development
        Report, 51–52
    Educational, Scientific and
        Cultural Organization
        (UNESCO), 54
    Food and Agriculture
        Organization, 25, 66, 67,
        109

Millennium Development
    Goals, 14, 53–54, 59

Wade, Abdoulaye, *110*
water, 14
Whitaker, Rosa, *116*
Wolfowitz, Paul, *116*
World Bank, 39, 53, 59, 62,
    63, 66, 89, 92–93, 96,
    116–117
The World Economy
    (Maddison), 62
World Trade Organization,
    111
World War I, 30

Zambia, 59, 73, 93
Zimbabwe, 56, 72, 94

PICTURE CREDITS

Page

2: Per-Anders Pettersson/Getty Images
9: © OTTN Publishing
12: Per-Anders Pettersson/Getty Images
18: R. Zurba/US AID
21: US AID
24: M. McGahuey/US AID
28: Library of Congress
31: Hulton-Deutsch Collection/Corbis
33: Tyler Hicks/Liaison/Getty Images
34: R. Zurba/US AID
38: Greg Marinovich/Getty Images
41: Alexander Joe/AFP/Getty Images
44: © OTTN Publishing
45: © OTTN Publishing
46: STR/AFP/Getty Images
49: Pius Utomi Ekpei/AFP/Getty Images
53: L. Lartigue/US AID
55: R. Zurba/US AID

57: © OTTN Publishing
58: WHO/TBP/Pierre Virot
62: C. Feezel/US AID
68: K. Stefanova/US AID
69: Peter Cunliffe-Jones/AFP/Getty Images
71: K. Burns/US AID
73: David McNew/Getty Images
75: Paul O'Driscoll/Getty Images
78: R. Zurba/US AID
80: US AID
85: R. Zurba/US AID
87: Eric Feferberg/AFP/Getty Images
90: E. Houston/US AID
95: L. Lartigue/US AID
98: US AID
107: Rajesh Jantilal/AFP/Getty Images
110: Panapress/Getty Images
113: Tim Graham/Getty Images
115: Sameh Sherif/AFP/Getty Images
116: Joe Raedle/Getty Images
120: C. Feezel/US AID

Front cover: Top Photos (left to right): K. Burns/US AID; K. Stefanova/US AID; S. Poland/US AID; Main Photo: Per-Anders Pettersson/Getty Images

Back cover: Collage of images created by OTTN Publishing with images provided by US AID

CONTRIBUTORS

PROFESSOR ROBERT I. ROTBERG is Director of the Program on Intrastate Conflict and Conflict Resolution at the Kennedy School, Harvard University, and President of the World Peace Foundation. He is the author of a number of books and articles on Africa, including *A Political History of Tropical Africa* and *Ending Autocracy, Enabling Democracy: The Tribulations of Southern Africa.*

TUNDE OBADINA, B.S., M.A., is a journalist and economist. He has worked for a number of organizations, including the British Broadcasting Corporation (BBC) and Reuters News agency. He is currently the director of Africa Business Information Service and is an external author for the Economist Intelligence Unit.

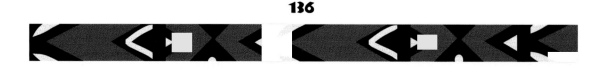

DATE DUE

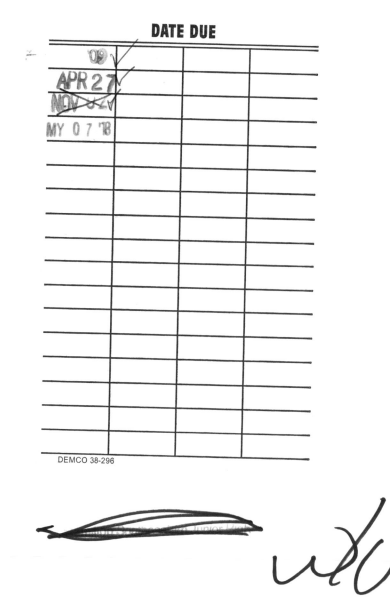

'09			
APR 27			
NOV			
MY 0 7 '18			

DEMCO 38-296